The Whale Oil Guards

THE
WHALE OIL GUARDS

BY

J. J. KENNEDY, D.S.O., C.F.

AUTHOR OF
"CARRIGMORE"; "THE INSEPARABLES";
"GORDON GRANDFIELD"; ETC.

The Naval & Military Press Ltd

Published by
The Naval & Military Press Ltd
5 Riverside, Brambleside, Bellbrook
Industrial Estate, Uckfield, East Sussex,
TN22 1QQ England

Tel: +44 (0) 1825 749494

Fax: +44 (0) 1825 765701

www.naval-military-press.com

www.military-genealogy.com

www.militarymaproom.com

In reprinting in facsimile from the original, any imperfections are inevitably reproduced and the quality may fall short of modern type and cartographic standards.

To the officers, non-commissioned officers and men of the A. I. F. with whom I was associated for several years, and especially to the members of the 14th Infantry Brigade, with unbounded admiration for their gallantry and deepest gratitude for their courtesy towards me at all times I affectionately dedicate this book.

                    JOHN J. KENNEDY.

October 30*th*, 1918.

PREFACE

AUSTRALIAN CORPS.

CORPS HEADQUARTERS,
21st December, 1918.

DEAR PADRE,

I have your letter of the 10th inst. with regard to the book you are writing for the 53rd Battalion. As I have, however, now left the Division to command the Australian Corps, I have sent your letter. with the attached document from Messrs. James Duffy & Co., to General Tivey, who now commands the 5th Australian Division, asking him to do what you wish if he can see his way to do so.

With regard to the 53rd Battalion, no words from me could fully convey what I feel is due to them for their magnificent gallantry during this year's fighting. During the Peronne operations, they did magnificent work, and accomplished what appeared to be almost the impossible. Notwithstanding their very severe losses on that occasion, within a month they were fit and ready again and engaged in fighting of the most desperate nature—with the most disastrous results to the Boche—

PREFACE.

in the capture of the Le Catelet System near Bellicourt, when the Division broke through the Hindenburg Line. All ranks of the Battalion have, throughout the time I have been associated with the Division, shown the greatest gallantry and devotion to duty, and, like their comrades in other Units of the Division, have never failed to accomplish the task that was given them, no matter how difficult the conditions were.

I should like to pay a tribute to the memory of their gallant Leader and Commander, the late Lieut.-Colonel Croshaw, D.S.O., who fell at the head of his Battalion at the Battle of Polygon Wood, September, 1917. No officer was ever prouder of his Battalion than Colonel Croshaw, and he, in no small measure, by his devotion, untiring energy, gallantry and example, made the Battalion the magnificent fighting machine that it has proved itself during the past months of long and strenuous fighting.

I wish you every success with your book, and will ask General Tivey to arrange to procure me a copy.

With very kindest regards and the Season's Greetings,

       I am,
          Yours sincerely,
             J. TALBOT HOBBS.

THE WHALE OIL GUARDS

THIS is a story of an Australian battalion. We Australians do not boast; therefore, though I may think it, I do not say it is the story of the bravest or the best Anzac battalion.

Incidentally, this is the story of Oswald Croshaw and other gallant men. Some have gone over the Great Divide and no crosses mark their graves. Others have gone Beyond, but white crosses mark their resting-places near the battle-line in the Western Front. A few have returned to Australia maimed and crippled. The medals they wear bear testimony to their gallantry. Let us hope that their countrymen will honour them for what they have dared and achieved, and that the Australian Government will be benignly zealous for the comfort of those battered heroes who have won glory for the Southern Cross.

SECTION I.

Major Oswald Croshaw was out of sorts. The desert had affected his nerves. Every mail from England brought him news of thrilling deeds and fierce encounters in France. The daily papers, belated indeed when they reached him, brought tidings of old school friends and mess-mates. Many had gained great honour and speedy advancement. The Major, though a military enthusiast, fretted and fumed in this lotus-land Egypt, while the Dogs of War cried havoc in Europe. History was being made. Men he had known and regarded as commonplace were now inscribing their names in golden letters on the scroll of fame, and here he must stagnate and dry-rot in this cursed desert.

"Brigade-Major to a yeomanry brigade doing garrison duty on the Canal! What an exciting job"! he thought while he chafed and cursed his ill-luck.

Oswald had formerly belonged to a crack Hussar regiment. He had seen service in South Africa during the Boer War. Unfortunately, he was too impetuous and outspoken to countenance injustice. Because he had protested indignantly against the persecution of a brother officer by an unscrupulous and vindictive C. O., he himself had incurred his Colonel's displeasure. That old scoundrel harassed the young captain so unceasingly, that Croshaw realized there was no career for him in the regiment, so he resigned his commission.

He married a charming Irish lady, amused himself with hunting and sport in England and Ireland, and was tolerably happy. But his heart was in soldiering. Hence, when the clarion cry of war sounded through the Empire, he gladly answered the call. He saw service on Gallipoli with a yeomanry regiment, and as a Major, then later Brigade-Major sojourned in Egypt after the famous evacuation of the Peninsula.

His Brigade was relegated to the Canal. Heat, flies, filth, niggers, and tainted bully-beef were the delights of each day. In the camp at Serapium the soldiers grew more discontented and more profane. His duties as Brigade-Major did not allow Croshaw to seek a change from the maddening monotony in Cairo or Alexandria. The best he could do in the way of recreation was a ride to the pretty Canal Company town—Ismailia. This place was truly an oasis in the desert. There was an excellent military club, a popular rendezvous for officers from Ferry Post, Moaska, Serapium and the other Canal stations.

It was a hot afternoon in March. Oswald had discovered that an old friend of his, now a Colonel, was on the staff of an Australian Division whose Headquarters were at Ferry Post. He was riding along the sand on his way to visit his old friend, and was agreeably impressed with the physique of thousands of Anzac soldiers who were bathing in the Canal.

" By Jove, what magnificent men ! "

He could not suppress this exclamation. Indeed the nude athletes who raced along the sand, or dived off the pier into the water, laughing and singing and jesting all the time, deserved the tribute he paid them. Brown and bronzed some of them, the lads who had erstwhile sparkled with the joy of life breasting the surf at Manly and Coogee, others were fair-skinned and more beautiful than sculpture in purest marble. All were vigorous and graceful as young Greek gods. Their muscles rippled in the sunlight as arms were waved and limbs were tossed in sport.

" How splendid," thought the Major. " It would be ripping to command a battalion of those fellows."

He found his friend, Colonel Wagstaffe, in his tent. The meeting after several years was pleasant for both. The Colonel called an orderly who returned immediately with refreshments. Over cigars and whiskey they discussed old times. Very soon the conversation veered round to current topics and their present activities.

Oswald Croshaw informed his old friend that he was "fed up" and bored to death. Wagstaffe on the contrary enthused about the Australians and his work in the Anzac Division to which he was attached.

"I say Croshaw, old chap! how about you throwing in your lot with us? You can negotiate the transfer easily. I shall speak to General Birdwood for you and get you a battalion later on. But for the present you must be content with a second in Command's job."

"There's nothing I should like better. I admired your chaps just now out there on the beach. Their physique is wonderful. I shall be eternally grateful if you can get me a transfer to your division."

"Right. It shall be done. Mind you, you must be careful in your attitude towards these Australians. They are all volunteers. Many of the men in the ranks are of independent means. You can't expect fróm them the convention, the servility, let me call it, of the English Tommy. But you will find them brave as lions in action, and always amenable to discipline if you treat them properly."

Major Croshaw laughed. "Yes, Wagstaffe, I have heard some queer yarns about their lack of discipline, but I daresay such tales are exaggerated."

"Perhaps not, Oswald. The Australian is a queer devil, and he does some queer things. He will never be over-awed by red tabs and sees no halo round the noble heads of staff-officers. General Birdwood, whom the men idolize, tells of an amusing experience he had on Gallipoli. He was walking along a certain sap one day, on his way to the line. A sentry was posted near an exposed part of the sap, particularly unhealthy, because Turkish snipers did not even let a sparrow twitter over it. The General was saluted very correctly by the sentry and with head erect proceeded carelessly on his way. But when he approached the dangerous gap the sentry hailed him in good Australian. "Duck, Birdie, you'd better b ——— well duck." The Generals to whom Sir William narrated this incident were shocked, outraged in fact. "What did you do?" they queried.

"What did I do?" he replied. "Why, I b ——— well ducked." "So you see, Croshaw, a sense of humour is indispensible when dealing with Australians."

The Major laughed very heartily at the anecdote. "I say!" he exclaimed, "I'm sure service with those chaps must be awfully jolly. Personally, while I realise the absolute necessity of discipline, I rather enjoy a departure from our stereotyped Tom Atkins."

"Well, my friend, I predict quite a great deal of enjoyment for you," the Colonel said with a meaning smile. For instance, I shan't be surprised if at your first appearance off parade in the Australian lines, when the Billjims behold your beautiful field boots and breeches, somebody whistles Pretty Joey. Or perhaps when they ascertain that you are a "Pommy" officer somebody will say : " Gie us a Woodbine, chum."

A few weeks later Oswald Croshaw accompanied by his groom Gibb, his servant Ramsay, frae Glasgie, and his dog Mena, reported to Colonel Norris, the C. O. of an Australian battalion. His appointment as Second in Command had already gone through orders. He found the Colonel a most courteous gentleman, a most conscientious officer, and a C. O. who welcomed to his command one so experienced in military science, as this regular cavalry-man was sure to be.

At mess he was introduced to the officers. They impressed him very favourably. All of them were young men, not a few mere boys just out of their teens. Their mirth was spontaneous, their manners easy, and their reception of him at once respectful and cordial. More than half were Gallipoli "veterans." These, of course unconsciously, often-times regarded themselves as superior to the reinforcement officers who had not yet been under fire. Quite a lot of good-natured banter was indulged in at the expense of the "cadets," as one young sub dubbed the recent arrivals.

Major Croshaw took up the cudgels in defence of the "unbaptized." "Never mind, gentlemen," he used to say. "This war will last long enough to make us all veterans. You Lone-Piners, should you be alive a year hence, will regard the Gallipoli stunts as mere cinema shows, compared with your experiences of war on the Western Front."

His words were uncannily prophetic as subsequent events proved.

The Senior Captain was evidently looked on as rather a scream by the officers. The M.O., a most charming and entertaining gentleman, took particular delight in drawing out this delightful three-pipper. The result was a delectable dissertation on Percy's favourite recreation in England, viz., leasing old baronial halls and living in them for periods ranging from one to three years. Of course we all believed him!

The redoubtable Percy was not Australian. He had been touring the Commonwealth at the outbreak of war, and eager for the fray, obtained a commission in a Light Horse Regiment. He was transferred to Colonel Norris's battalion a few weeks before Major Croshaw's arrival at Ferry Post.

After mess, being rather tired, Oswald retired to his tent. Groups of men were returning from the Y. M. C. A. hut and the canteens down the road. Some were discussing the war in a most intelligent and educated manner. Others talked about their bush experiences in Australia. Some sang gems of classical songs with voices that showed fine quality, and fine expression, evidently the result of much training. Others again sang weird melodramatic stuff that could scarce be called beautiful. In a tent not far from Croshaw's, the occupants had organized an impromptu concert. A man named " Snowy " responded to a command from the master of the revels by playing on the violin in a most delightfully artistic style several operatic selections. A " bloke " who answered to the appellation of Bluey Duffal, rendered with much prolonged nasal pathos " The Face on the Bar-room floor." The heroine of the song was compelled by the poet to rhyme with floor, so her virtue was not any better than it ought have been.

" By Jove ! " thought the new Second in

Command. "What an extraordinary mixture of cultured men and extremes of the other sort! But how droll and refreshing the devils are!"

With which pious reflection, more content and light-hearted than he had been for months, Oswald Croshaw turned over and slept the sleep of the physically healthy.

SECTION II.

The Green and Blacks, so called after their regimental colours, very soon realized the presence of Major Croshaw among them. He looked a soldier every inch, and though the men had no very pleasant memories of their associations with English officers on Gallipoli, they admired him though a "Pommy" as he walked through the lines or rode round the parade-ground to inspect their training. The slackers soon discovered his keenness, and bestirred themselves. The men who loved the game of soldiering recognised in him an officer after their own hearts, in fact a military enthusiast.

A lecture by him to the N.C.O's soon after his arrival will be remembered as long as the battalion exists. One admonition particularly was appreciated and acted on, as subsequent events proved :—" The reputation of this battalion is in the making. Its future depends on you. It is for you to see to it whether in years to come we shall be spoken of as *The Green and Blacks* or the poor old Green and Blacks."

His job was by no means a sinecure, nor was his temper entirely equable, so that in those first months of his career with Australians, before he understood them, he flared up rather frequently. On those occasions his sarcasm was so cutting that officers sometimes voted him a beast and men a bastard (that choice Australian epithet which may sometimes in their mouths be complimentary. The writer has over-heard himself described by the men as a decent old bastard).

The Major commented on the frequent use of this opprobrious epithet, when discussing matters regimental one evening with Captain Arblaster.

" Look here, Arblaster, these men are no whit worse than Tommies as regards profanity. In fact I must say to their credit that they are rarely blasphemous, but I wish you fellows could get them to cut out that awful word."

" Well, Sir, we have tried our hardest, but we don't seem to succeed. For myself I must confess I am no longer shocked by their lurid language. I have seen them on the Peninsula charging as only heroes can charge in the face of fearful odds. Their language then was sulphurous, but their hearts were hearts of oak and their self-sacrifice and fearlessness wonderful. I wouldn't worry, Sir, about this matter, let the Padres deal with it."

"The best sermon on profanity I have ever heard was from a famous Roman Catholic priest, whose gallantry on Gallipoli made him the idol of the troops. Would you like to hear it, Sir ? It's very short " Captain Jock Thompson asked.

"Let's have it, Thompson ! I hope its done *you* good," the Major replied.

The officers laughed loudly. Jock Thompson, a redoubtable Scotchman was a darned good soldier, but his profanity on occasions was a thousand candle-power.

"Well, Sir, the Brigadier asked Father ——— to lecture the men on the language abuse. The Padre did it in this way : 'Look here, ye devils, I want ye to moderate your language. I say cut out that awful word f———. The first bastard I hear using it, I won't crime him, but I'll punch air-holes through his crimson carcase.' Let me assure you, Sir, the banned word was largely discontinued."

Major Croshaw almost collapsed with

laughter. In fact so overwhelming was Jock's yarn that Doc. Cosgrove, the mess president, fined the narrator. The penalty was drinks all round.

Captain Harry Pauline must have been eager to pay for another round of Johnny Walker. Captain Pauline, or Ironsides as the Padre christened him, told a tale of a certain Turkish war-correspondent. This Mahomeddan, Philip Gibbs, describing in a Stamboul paper the Lone Pine battle, wrote a vivid account of the affair, which being translated reads as follows :—" Australians charged madly up the heights calling loudly on their great god BASTARD."

Some god !! Some Australians !!!

The weeks dragged on, and still General McCay's division was detained in Egypt. The men cursed Ferry Post. They consigned to the infernal regions the desert and its devilish belongings. Tortured by Kamseens, by flies (who has campaigned in Egypt and has not suffered agonies from these ubiquitous multitudinous and ravening pests ?) by fierce burning heat, by all the plagues that even now infest the land of the Pharaohs, the men grew querulous and discontented. Route marches were the order of the day. Marching over arid desert and drifting sand in the glare of the relentless sun was bad enough, but the orders always insisted on full packs and equipment and the consequent strain brought many soldiers to the limit of endurance.

On the 15th May, 1916, the battalion marched to Hogg's Back, where we assumed garrison duties along a section of the Canal defence trenches.

Though Hogg's Back was desert with a vengeance, it was vastly preferable to Ferry Post. There was no route marching out here, so the fortnight spent in this section was rather a rest. The weather was exceptionally hot even for that accursed clime, but the sand was not fouled, the camp was clean, and consequently the fly pest was not so palpable. After sunset each evening the air was cooler and fresher. Then the men sprawled on the sand near their tents ; some smoked, others sky-larked, and others disturbed the peace that broods over the desert singing the songs our soldiers love.

The Major enjoyed those evenings. The Colonel, Captain Cosgrove, the M.O., Father Kennedy, Lieut. Pearson, the Q.M. Lieut. Moffit, the Adjutant, and one or two of the Company Commanders invariably foregathered outside the mess-tent when the twilight set in. Croshaw learned a great deal about Australian life while he listened to those officers indulge in reminiscences or discuss the politics and the social activities of the Sunny South.

Rumour had it that the division would embark for France within a fortnight, hence the anticipation of real soldiering in the Western Front roused officers and men from the lethargic discontent that had of late beset them. A new Brigadier—Colonel Pope, of Gallipoli renown—had been appointed to the Green Brigade. He was a hearty bluff Australian. The men swore by him because he was assiduous in visiting not only every battalion, but every company daily, speaking words of encouragement to the Anzacs, and promising them stirring times in the near future.

While at Hogg's Back the Padre wrote a few verses which he arranged to the music of a popular marching song. Major Croshaw had many copies typed in the orderly-room. The men learnt the lines quickly, and made it their battalion war-song.

'Tis purple dawn on the desert sand,
  So rise from dreams of your Southern Land.
The bugle calls, we must march away
  Soldiers of young Australia,
We are the boys of the —— 3rd.
  Brave lads amongst us have fought and heard
The thunders of war at the Dardanelles,
  Let us march to avenge our comrades.

(Chorus).

Marching for Australia's glory,
  Marching away to France,
We have tramped and toiled through the
    desert,
  Hark to our proud advance.
Cheerily through scenes we hated,
  In the land that Moses cursed,
At last we shall strike a blow, lads,
  So cheer up —— thirds.

'Twas weary marching from Tel-el-keber,
  The months since then were dark and
    drear,
Free sons of the Sunny Southern Land
  We loathed those fawning niggers.
But to sand and flies and camels too
  To grinning hinds of the Effindi crew,
To the heat and filth of this horrid land
  To-day we shall cry out—Imshi!

(Chorus).

Marching for Australia's glory,
  Marching away to France,
To the land of smiling vinyards,
  Hark to our proud advance.
Cheerily through scenes we hated,
Madly will the Kaiser curse
  When our Green and Black will be
    honoured,
    So cheer up —— Thirds.

Those days were pleasant enough. Many a comical jest and amusing practical joke made life worth living. The Padre and the Doctor were never too dull to indulge in side-splitting anecdotes. or breezy repartee. Poor old Ironsides—Captain Pauline must have appreciated the society of the Headquarters people, for he rarely absented himself from their soirées. The Colonel on one occasion announced at the mess that he wished to see Pauline on regimental business. The Adjutant called an Orderly and was about to send him to instruct Captain Pauline to report at headquarters, when Captain Cosgrove interfered.

"There's no need to send an orderly, Moffit, I can get him here far more expeditiously. With your permission, Colonel, I will draw the cork of one of those bottles of Bass. I guarantee if Pauline is anywhere within a five-mile radius, he will be here in ten minutes. He's got a truly remarkable, in fact, a phenomenal nose."

The Colonel consented. Ironsides reported within five minutes. His face reflected the Purple East. His tongue was incontinent and careened out of his mouth in unctuous lickings and smackings. 'Twas the delight of anticipation.

Poor Harry Pauline, what a magnificent giant he was! How good humouredly he put up with all our chaff and banter!

Among the men in those days there were some extraordinary characters.

There was Corporal Duffal, the man whose repertoire included the weirdest collection of Australian come-all-you's.

There was wee Peter, a Malay, whose knowledge of English was very limited, consequently his vocabulary, learned in the lines from men who didn't teach him exactly classical Anglo-Saxon, was startling in the extreme. Peter while we were at Hogg's Back suffered from diarrhœa. He paraded to the doctor. Questioned by Captain Cosgrove as to his indisposition and its symptoms Peter upset the gravity of the Medical Tent by exclaiming, " Sir, I gotta the ———! " Well, he didn't call the malady diarrhœa.

There were the cooks, or the "babbling brooks," as the men called them. Invariably greasy, sooty, and begrimed, they were as kind-hearted as women, and worked might and main to make the camp fare appetizing and attractive.

There was Bluey Ward, the Q. M's batman. Why he was called Bluey, Major Croshaw could not understand, for Ward's hair was a fiery red, and his face gave testimony to oceans of Australian beer that must have flowed down his weather-beaten neck.

Bluey was incorrigible. He had many

lapses from grace, but Captain Pearson condoned each offence. The climax came at Hogg's Back. Pearson sent the redoubtable Bluey one day from the Rail Head to deliver a verbal message to the Adjutant. The weather was beastly hot. On the way to the camp the messenger slaked his tormenting thirst at a beer canteen. He imbibed not wisely but too well. The Adjutant was in his tent enjoying half-an-hour's siesta, when the beer-soaked Mercury arrived. He endeavoured to deliver the message, but the weary Adjutant referred him to the orderly-room, or to hell, whereupon Bluey, eager to vindicate the slightest affront to his master's dignity, tweaked the Adjutant's nose. Bluey's dormitory that night was the guard-tent. His career as batman likewise ended.

After this serious lapse, poor Ward's crime-sheet became voluminous. The Major looked on him as rather a " bad hat." Not all the kindly advice of the Padre nor the vigilance of Q. M. S. Campbell, the best-natured and most unselfish man in the battalion, could keep the unfortunate Bluey out of trouble.

On the 30th May, the Green and Blacks were relieved by an English regiment. Officers and men were in excellent spirits as they marched back to Ferry Post. We simmered here for another fortnight, but were cheery none the less, for we had received definite orders to prepare for embarkation. We marched to Moasca on the 16th June, and entrained for Alexandria on the 18th.

What a memorable trip it was! The men were crowded in open trucks. The officers' trucks were just as congested. The old train bumped and jolted and jogged, but we did not mind. We were leaving Egypt; very soon we would be in La Belle France, and what cared we for death or danger when there was fighting to be done! All night long we rattled towards the port, but sleep did not worry us. We sang and jested and laughed. We shared our flasks and the parcels which provident batmen had procured us. The C. O. was as gay and light-hearted as the most junior sub. As for Oswald Croshaw, well he threatened to place under arrest any officer caught napping or neglecting to swell with his voice the merry chorus.

What a mercy from God is this infectious mirth, this schoolboy hilarity, so characteristic of our soldiers! If reason urged on us the imminence of fierce struggles and bloody experiences, we refused to entertain the prospect, and with utter joy in the present made our motto—" Laugh and make merry."

SECTION III.

On the 19th of June, at 7 a.m., we embarked at Alexandria on the good ship *The Royal George*.

This transport had been, before the war, a liner "de luxe," specially built for those British and American plutocrats who follow the summer, so to speak. Having escaped the inclemency of the Northern Winter, they used to enjoy life on the Riviera and then cross on gilded floating palaces, such as this ship of ours, to love and revel, flirt and intrigue at Cairo, Luxor, Assouan, and other enchanted cities of the Purple East.

On this boat the men had very comfortable quarters. As for the officers, they lived in luxurious state-cabins. Every two officers shared a suite comprising bed-room, sitting-room and bath-room. The catering, too, was excellent.

What a change from the fly-infested camps of Egypt!

Constant companionship with Oswald Croshaw during that most pleasant of voyages gave me a complete understanding of the man's nature. There were many matters about which we differed, but these clashings of opinions and beliefs did not impair our friendship one whit. I learnt to recognise in him the enthusiastic soldier whose first consideration was his country's cause, the generous patriot who loved his England so dearly that he waxed angry when he spoke of the politicians and traffickers whose show of disinterestedness was so thinly disguised, whose lust for place and position made them our most dangerous and insidious foes.

Owing to some menace out at sea, probably enemy submarines, we did not move out of harbour until the 22nd of June. But we did not mind. Our life on the ship was so restful and comfortable that we regarded it as a delightful holiday, and each day of delay was a much-appreciated extension. Deck sports were the order of the day. Concerts and card-parties whiled away the evenings. The three other battalions of our brigade were on board transports anchored near us. Colonel Norris for some reason refused to allow our men swim, probably he feared they might swim back to Australia. The other C. O's were not so strict, and so their soldiers every afternoon while we remained at anchor swarmed down the sides of their ships and enjoyed themselves to their hearts' content in the water. Some of them used to paddle over to us, and, with a "Hello digger," start chaff and repartee with their mates on *The Royal George*. They professed to bring us the latest news. Just as well for the Kaiser that the various happenings announced with regard to him weren't facts. Otherwise he would have been a very much-abused and tortured monarch. We were also informed that Tasmania had sent an ultimatum to King Island, that it had declared war on the Commonwealth, that the Tight Little Island was now a republic, and King O'Malley had abdicated and retired to his retreat at Collingwood.

The First Class Dining Saloon was a place of revelry during the officers' mess hours. I shall never forget our particular party. We foregathered before the first meal on the boat and secured a table to ourselves. There were the writer, Captain Cosgrove, Captain Harry Pauline, Lieut. Johnson and Lieut. Pearson. None of us were wowsers, we all had a sense of humour. The M. O., Captain Cosgrove, was the best mimic and raconteur in our mess; Captain Pauline's good humour never flagged, in fact it became more infectious after he'd had several whiskies. Johnson (Uncle John with the bloodshot voice) was one of the driest wits in our battalion. Pearson a regular Beau Nash lent tone to our particular table, and the wirter, sure he was Irish, therefore

irrepressible. Oswald Croshaw, as Second in
Command, had of course to sit at the King
Table with the Heads, but he often cast
wistful glances towards our merry party.
Reader, please don't think we caroused not
wisely but too well. We never exceeded the
limit, not even Harry Pauline, whose absorbing
properties were phenomenal, though Mr.
Johnson doth allege that Ironsides turned into
his bath instead of his bunk one night and
slumbered there till morning.

On the morning of the 22nd we put out to
sea. We were escorted during the voyage by
a destroyer. The weather was excellent, and
the trip across the Mediterranean uneventful.
On the last day we steamed close to the shore.
The scenery was entrancing, and became more
lovely as we approached our destination. The
city of Marseilles, with its tiers of streets
rising picturesquely from the water's edge, the
soft tints of faded brick buildings and moss-clad
tiled roofs, interspersed with the rich green of
beautiful trees in full foliage, the old-time
monuments, the gloriously situated Church of
Notre Dame crowning the heights, its golden
Madonna looking out over the sea, all combined
to form a lovely picture indeed.

We arrived at Marseilles on the 26th of
June, and entrained for the North on the 27th.
The troop-train was slow but comfortable.

It took us three days to get to our destination, but we were not at all tired. Indeed, this slow mode of travelling was an advantage, for we had an excellent opportunity to see the country. As the train steamed along, our eyes feasted on the loveliness of La Belle France. Beautifully cultivated farms, magnificent chateaus, serpentine rivers, castled crags, gray old towns with their old-time cathedrals and abbeys, picture succeeded picture and outrivalled it in beauty, so that we grudged to nature the hours of sleep, when night flung a dark mantle over this rich and fair land. The towns along the route were old and historic; Avignon, once the refuge of the exiled Popes, Tresancon, Orange, and many other places of interest. Everywhere along the way the people cheered us and blessed us. Many a time I noticed among the smiling young girls and the laughing children women in the deepest mourning. They were the young widows and the aged mothers who mourned for brave men who would never return to them. Even while their voices blessed us, the salt tears of sorrow coursed down their sad pallid faces.

The Quarter Master attended most efficiently to the feeding of the troops during those few days. Certain places were laid down as halts where the troop train stopped and the men descended from the cars to obtain rations of tea and provisions. Hot water was always ready at these places, so the cooks got busy, and in an incredibly short time the mess orderlies had steaming dishes of tea to dispense to the soldiers. Of course some of our lads supplemented their rations with fruit, cake, and " vin rogue," purchased at the station buffets.

We officers had some jolly scraps for refreshments at these stopping-places. Major Croshaw, Doctor Cosgrove, Lieut. Pearson and I had a compartment to ourselves. The Major and his trusty henchman, Ramsay from Gleskatoon, were extraordinary foragers, no whit better though than my prince of batmen, Dick Harrison, so we fared most sumptuously. Ah me, what a merry quartet we were. All four of us had trotted round this old globe to some effect, so what with tales of our adventures and experiences, we did not lack entertainment. Yet if we only knew, tragedy and disaster were only some weeks ahead in the veiled future.

There was never a better Anzac battalion than ours. The men and the N. C. O's were keen and eager. The officers—alack, not many of them are left now—were splendid types of gallant Australian manhood.

The four Company Commanders, Major Samson, Captains Thomson, Arblaster and

Murray, were conscientious officers, popular and respected by their subalterns and their men.

Charley Arblaster, though only twenty-one, was my ideal officer. He was a clean-cut athletic and handsome fellow. He had graduated and obtained his commission at Duntroon military college, had served with the Light Horse on Gallipoli, and obtained speedy promotion. He had been wounded some time before the evacuation, and was sent to England to convalesce. When he returned to Egypt he applied for and was granted a transfer to the infantry. Had he been spared his career as a soldier would be a brilliant one. His company was the crack company, the best disciplined, and the most competent in every respect. He was a born leader of men. His influence over them was largely due to his cleanliness of life and his rectitude in all his dealings.

The subs were a good lot. Boys in years, they were boys too as far as animal spirits and a healthy joy of life went, but they were men in this respect: they realized their responsibilities as officers, and did their utmost to be true to their trust. Of course they were not perfect. The C. O. and Major Croshaw found it necessary to strafe them now and then, but it did them good.

When near Paris the train branched off, much to our disappointment, as we had hoped to see the gay city. We had steamed slowly through some of its suburbs on the banks of the lovely Seine. These glimpses were so delightful that we were eager to see the city itself with its boulevards and gardens. However, we were disappointed. Night came on and again obscured the view, but next morning we found ourselves near the Channel. We strained our eyes for a glimpse of the white cliffs of Albion. Our route lay through Boulogne, Calais, Saint Omer and Hazebrouck. At 4.30 p.m. on the 30th of June, we detrained near a village called Thiennes and marched to our billets in the neighbourhood.

We shall never forget Thiennes nor the kindness of the good French people among whom we were first billeted. All ranks were comfortably housed. The six Headquarters officers were allotted rooms " chez Monsieur Dave," a wine merchant. The doctor and I were shown the room upstairs which we were to share. Cosgrove, on mischief bent, found a diminutive bowler hat which he donned. The effect was funny in the extreme. He looked exactly like Charlie Chaplin, and as he had made a study of the celebrity, he went to the window and entertained our boys waiting on the road with some Chaplin turns.

Loud cheers and laughter, and cries of "More, Doc.! Give us more!"

Madame and Mademoiselle Dave were very kind to us. It was marvellous how Darby, the H. Q. Mess cook, and Sergeant Gallagher, the caterer, made themselves understood and after a few hours had established themselves in the kitchen. The same Darby was some character.

Didn't our boys enjoy the "vin." Our stay meant a golden harvest to old Dave with the bulbous rubicund nose. The old scoundrel had the time of his life, but the unfortunate dog that used to drag the wine cart to replenish the neighbouring estaminets supplied by our host was worked overtime.

I say, Captain Cosgrove! should you read these memoirs, you will remember the night your room-mate flashed an electric torch on old Dave after we had been disturbed by weird gruntings and objurgations coming from the yard below. What a revelation the flashlight disclosed, and what a fright we gave the old sinner! Monsieur Dave, very drunk and very dishabille, was seized with such terror because of that bright beam of light that he started to run round in circles like the Blind One on the Nikko Road, that queer devil-ridden character of H. De Vere Stackpoole's tale, "The Crimson Azaleas."

We were proud of our boys during our stay at Thiennes. Every evening after mess Major Croshaw, Captains Cosgrove, Kennedy, and Pauline, used to stroll through the fields and woods and enjoy to their hearts' content the peace and beauty of this lovely bit of rural France. During such walks they met Australian lads everywhere in happy intercourse with the kindly peasant folk. The men were gentlemanly and chivalrous in their relations with the women and girls ; they delighted to assist them in their work—milking the cows, cutting green fodder, or drawing water from the wells. Our experience then was confirmed often afterwards. Put our Australian soldiers among good women who respect themselves and never will they behave other than Christians and gentlemen.

Those evening walks were full of interest. The sweet golden-haired children played with us and were not at all shy. We helped them to pull wild flowers to place at the feet of the Madonnas in the way-side shrines. All the time the booming of big guns rumbled sullenly in the distance. Now and again aerial combats took place almost over our heads. Puffs of shrapnel floated high in the air round the reconnoitring Hun planes, and our machines, like circling falcons, mounted in spirals to grapple with the winged enemy and bring him down or send him back behind his lines.

Yes, Thiennes was a pleasant place! But, alas, all good things here below come to an end, so did our sojourn in this French Arcadia. Saturday, July the 8th, was our last day here, for the order to move forward had been issued to our Brigade. We sniffed battle in the air, but we sang and laughed and made the welkin ring that last evening of our stay among the friendly rustics of Thiennes.

SECTION IV.

On the morning of the 9th of July, the Green Brigade marched to the forward area. Our route lay through the town of Merville. The march, though rather long and over rough cobble roads, was successfully accomplished, the march discipline was excellent and there were no stragglers. We compared very favourably with the other battalions of our brigade in this move. The brigade as a whole was complimented on its success, while the other brigades of our division were strafed rather severely by the G. O. C.

We were billeted two days near Estaires. These billets were our first experience of the inevitable quadrangular farm-house with the rectangular stink, as Bairnsfather describes it, in the centre. The people in this district were neither so amiable nor so clean as our friends at Thiennes. Alack, no longer did we have the luxury of beds, we officers, had to unroll our valises and sleep on the hard stone floors.

On the 11th July, we marched out from Estaires at 8.30 p.m. We marched through Sailly, to Fleurbaix, near which town two of our battalions took over the front line of trenches, and two of our companies had their first experience of the support trenches.

I shall never forget that march. It was dusk when we passed through Sailly. Its church and many of its buildings had been shelled and destroyed. We looked with awe on these ruined houses, and trudged on out of the town. Now we realized that we were near the firing-line. Flares, bright and incandescent, were being continuously flung up in the air. The crack of rifle-fire hammered an ominous staccatto. More venomous still sounded the machine guns. Behind and in front of us were numerous guns which crashed and flashed fire as they hurled their terrible projectiles—their messengers of ruin and death—towards the enemy's position. In answer to them Fritz's guns roared in the distance, and his shells shrieked over our heads. Sometimes a shell burst near us, the earth staggered 'neath the blow, and a column of clay and smoke arose high in the air. Fortunately, the road escaped, so we had no casualties. At last we entered the semi-ruined town of Fleurbaix. Two of our companies marched further on to the support trenches. The other companies were fooled and muddled about, owing to the congestion of troops in the place and the damnable delay on the part of the people we relieved in moving out. Just as well for us that the Hun didn't know of the relief taking place in Fleurbaix that night, or he would have blown us out of existence.

'Twas 3 a.m. when the Headquarters officers finally settled in their billets.

Oswald Croshaw turned in at 4 a.m., so tired and exhausted, that neither the roaring of the guns, nor the hissing of the enemy shells worried him much.

Most of us slept as soundly and as deeply as if we were a hundred miles behind the firing-line.

Fleurbaix was interesting, though not a health resort.

The church, a fine building, had been badly shelled, but was still in a fair state of preservation.

Despite the daily bombardments of the place,

there were still many French civilians in the town. Several estaminets did a roaring trade. Other haunts very popular with us lads were the tea-shops, where enterprising madames sold eggs and chips to the Billjims.

The legend on one of the windows was rather amusing: "English spoken, Australian understood."

Our headquarters billet was a fine house at the far end of the street opposite the town hall. Though the buildings on each side of it had suffered more or less severely, this residence had never been touched. Major Croshaw used to warn us that some day in the near future a shell would come crashing through it and give the knock-out blow to several or many of us, but we laughed and declared that a ticket to Eternity or Blighty at this early stage would be stiff luck indeed.

Our mess-room could hardly be called shell-proof. The roof was glass, but even when the shells flitted dangerously low of an evening, we smoked there unconcernedly, and continued our game of bridge with as much zest and enjoyment, as if we whiled away the leisure hours in the safe and sumptuous lounges of the Hotel Australia or Scott's.

Our companies in the support trenches were shelled occasionally during their stay, but there were no casualties.

We used to visit these companies every day. Some of us officers wended our way to the Front line daily, as we expected to relieve one of our battalions in their particular sector.

Though the enemy shelled Fleurbaix almost every evening, we escaped casualties. Other units in the town—English Engineers and Artillery—lost men every day. Round the church was especially unhealthy.

Captain Cosgrove and Father Kennedy had rather a narrow shave on their way to the Brigade Machine Gun Headquarters, where they had promised to dine. When sauntering leisurely by the church a shell burst some yards from them. Neither of them suffered injury, though three men a yard or two further from the place were hit by shell fragments. One was killed instantaneously, the other two had serious head and body wounds.

The Padre reckoned they were immune after that experience. The doctor thanked God that he was spared to enjoy Tom Dick's whiskey. A Billjim, sauntering by with hands in his breeches pockets, made the statement that shells were nasty things and made a very untidy mess, but he didn't give a continental.

That was some evening at Captain Dick's, believe me!

Early on the morning of the 15th of July we were advised that we would march out of Fleurbaix that evening to another part of the line. We were not informed of it generally, but every man in the battalion knew that our division was to do a big thing in the very near future.

Before the march out Fritz started a heavy bombardment. The in-coming regiment was very late, so we were detained a long time. There were no fewer than three gas alarms in an hour, so we juggled our faces into the masks, and sweated and cursed the Hun and his hell-inspired methods of warfare. At last we moved out about 10 p.m. to billets near Bac-St-Maur. I was summoned away to minister to two English lads who had been wounded. When I returned my trusty attendant, Dick, was seated on my valise outside a wooden hut. He informed me that the officers were ranged like sardines in a box in this shed, that they were all asleep, and there was no room for me. We groped round, found a lean-to shieling near the farm-house close by, also discovered clean straw. We spread this liberally on the floor of the place. Dick unrolled my valise. Darby, the Headquarters cook, Sergeant Gallagher, Dick and I shared this sleeping apartment. Judging by the snores from my bed companions, they were sleeping all right. I soon followed suit, and never slept better. Next morning, about 4 a.m., I was aroused by sundry ungentle digs in the small of my back, and awoke indignantly to find a formidable sow shoving me about with her snout. Well, 'twas time to get up I thought, so I arose and exit Madame Pig.

That morning, Sunday, July 16th, we were instructed to be ready for a move to the front-line trenches after night-fall. Church parades were arranged, and the boys most earnestly commended themselves to God for help and courage to do their duty in the coming battle.

All day long Father Kennedy was kept busy (after Mass) hearing confessions in an open field. The earnestness shown by the R. C. soldiers on this occasion made a great impression on Oswald Croshaw. He noted in his commanding officer, Colonel Norris, in several of the officers who were Catholics too, and in many of the men, a wonderful exhilaration and readiness for anything that might befall after they had interviewed their priest and made their peace with God.

Just before we moved into the line we received news that distressed us sorely. Major Croshaw was attached to the Brigade Staff as forward Brigade Major for the coming stunt. Oswald was at first furious, but well, there was this consolation, he would be right in the affair after all, and there was no use grumbling. So on reflection he calmed down, shrugged his shoulders, and said "C'est la guerre."

We marched forward at 9.30 p.m. under a cold drizzling mist. We took over a section of the line from the Reds and Blacks of the Red Brigade of our Division. A and B companies occupied the front line. C and D, with battalion Headquarters, were in supports. We experienced one of the delights of a relief, found another battalion Headquarters occupying the shelters and dug-outs supposed to be ours. Likewise another delight, the Aid post existed only in name. The Colonel and the Adjutant, with their orderly-room staff, occupied the space between all that was left of the four walls of a brick house, and carried on there. The doctor and I sat on the ground in the open, with our backs against an old brick wall. This wall was bullet-proof. Those marvellous fellows, Dick and old James, provided us with hot tea through the night. Captain Tom Dick joined us. We smoked a while, told yarns a while, and though machine-gun bullets hissed and whistled round, or cracked the old brick wall at our backs, we—strange to relate—slept a while. Then towards dawn, we were summoned to our first casualty

Lieutenant Lang, wounded before on Gallipoli, received his second crack or souvenir of the great war—a bullet below the knee. A nice Blighty, his fellow-officers said, but Long Jo was a fire-eater, and cursed his ill-luck.

How the Colonel endeared himself to the men during those days. There was no rest for him. Several times a day he visited the front line, and even when shells were bursting perilously near, he carried on conversation with the officers. His men were his chief care. For all of them he had a smile and a cheery word of greeting. I often heard during those trying days before the battle such scraps of conversation as these :

"I say, digger! Isn't the old man the goods ? "

"You've just said it, cobber! He'll do me, and I'm hard to please!"

All day, through the 17th of July, our artillery was very active. The enemy, too, shelled us pretty heavily. Hence there were many casualties, and we were kept going at the Aid Post. Our A. M. C. boys lived in this shelter, so when things were quiet and there were no wounded to be attended to, Captain Cosgrove and I came down to our brick wall. The day was warm and bright, and we enjoyed our little piece of earth.

On the 18th of July, the firing was heavy

all day. We had more casualties than on the previous day, but comparatively few from our own battalion. Towards evening we took over from the Green and Purples the section occupied by them. The night was fairly quiet, but two beastly gas-alarms disturbed our rest.

During the night the Colonel sent for me. He was well-nigh exhausted from want of sleep, but cheery and bright. Nevertheless, he was doubtful as to the issue of the coming scrap.

"Look here," he said to me, " this affair has been deferred too long. I have no doubt as to how my men will shape. God bless them, they are splendid, but I fear our efforts will be in vain. Why ! the civilians behind the lines are asking : ' When is the big attack to come off ' ? When this is so, you may be certain Fritz knows there's something in the wind, and he will be prepared."

"The staff work doesn't impress me," I replied. "Orders are issued and cancelled again so often that it seems to me there's a hopeless muddle."

"That's just what I fear, my friend," he answered. "The blame doesn't lie with our Divisional Staff. Croshaw informed me a while ago that, what with orders and counter-orders, they are completely dazed down at

Brigade and D. H. Q. Poor Croshaw hasn't had half-an-hour's rest since Sunday. The same is true of all of us, but we will do our job. I only wish they would give the order and not wear out the men with this uncertainty."

Major Croshaw's entry interrupted our conversation.

"Well, Colonel," he announced, "to-morrow's the day. Thank God. Another day's delay and I should be fit for the madhouse. The dispositions will be given to the Battalion Commanders to-morrow morning at a meeting of C. O's at Brigade. The G. hasn't yet decided on the hour, but you will be notified. How are things, Sir?"

"Everything's all right, Croshaw. Sorry old chap you shan't be with us in our particular part of the fray. But never mind."

"Good-night, Sir, and good-luck."

Major Croshaw saluted, and hastened away to the other battalions.

"Thank God we've got something definite at last," Colonel Norris exclaimed. "F ——— do you believe in presentiments?"

"Well, Sir, I have never experienced any, so I am not in a position to answer your question," I replied.

"Neither have I been troubled with presentiments before now. But to-day, even this very moment, I feel almost convinced that tomorrow will witness ny first and last fight. Strange to say, the thought does not worry me until I think of Bessie and my child. My God, if ever a man were blessed with a perfect wife, I am. Perhaps we are too happy. Should anything happen me! I mean should the worst befall, will you write to her?"

Here the Colonel's emotion choked his words. I tried to laugh at his fears.

"Nonsense, Colonel. Put the silly thought out of your head. The battalion is bound to do great things to-morrow. And you, why you will come out of the scrap unscathed! The next thing for you will be a D.S.O., or a C.M.G., and what a proud woman your wife will be. You can rely on me, Sir, should anything untoward happen, to write to her and comfort her as best I can. Meantime, you have your Faith, let it comfort you."

We clasped hands as men do who are friends n times of crisis. Then I was called away. I bade Colonel Norris good-night. I saw him again next morning in the line. The priest had assembled a number of Catholics who wished to receive Holy Communion before the Hop Over. They were kneeling along the head of the communication trench. One of them was Colonel Norris. He was the first to receive the August Sacrament. His head was bent back as the Padre administered the Sacred Host, and on his face was the rapt expression of a saint, of a soldier of Christ, who has glimpsed the glory of the Great Beyond. After that I saw him no more.

SECTION V.

Soldiers of my old battalion, men of my old brigade, comrades of my old division, this chapter tells of a day we can never forget; it recalls an event in our history at once glorious and terrible, a battle that was a defeat and at the same time a magnificent victory.

The Nineteenth of July, 1916! The date will be written in letters of blood in the annals of our battalion. Fromelles! In years to come those who will carry on the glorious traditions of the Green and Blacks will salute the name and be inspired by the memory of our heroes who died in that battle.

In the early morning a tremendous deafening and bewildering artillery demonstration was inaugurated. Long-range guns of gigantic calibre miles and miles back, hundreds of great guns of shorter range, thousands of field guns, all belched their terrible missiles into the enemy lines that were to be our objectives. The effect was stunning, paralysing. But if the mere crash and roar and tumult of these demons of death thrilled us, what must have been the effect on the enemy and their cataclysmic destruction of the enemy's ramparts and defences ?

The German guns retaliated not so vigorously, but still their bombardment of our tranches was indeed drastic.

I walked along the front and support lines that morning. Shells burst perilously near, and very often I paused to attend to our dying and injured lads on their way to the Aid Posts.

At 3 p.m., the Green and Purples again took over the left 300 yards of our trenches. We closed in on our original front of 300 yards with the River L——— on our right. A and B companies, under Captains Thompson and Murray, were in the front line. C and D companies, under Major Sampson and Captain Arblaster, were in the support trenches.

The battalion moved to attack the German line in four waves. One half of A and one half of B formed the first wave. The other halves of A and B, the second half of C and D constituted the third wave. The remainder of C and D with the battalion headquarters made the fourth wave.

The first wave hopped over at 5.43 p.m.,

followed by the second wave at a distance of one hundred yards. Both waves reached the German wire, here they lay down until 6 p.m. They then charged gallantly with a fine dash and an irresistible impetuosity. They were followed by the third and fourth waves. We bayoneted or bombed the enemy who garrisoned the line, and after a sharp but short struggle, captured their first and second lines. Bombing parties advanced two hundred yards further, in order to hold back the Fritz bombers who were counter-attacking on the front and the right flank. The remainder of our men proceeded to consolidate our position in the captured German first and second lines.

Already our losses were severe. Among the fallen was our gallant Colonel. He was leading his wave on to the second line, calling out to his men to follow and deal it to the blighters, when a deadly spray of machine-gun bullets from the right flank riddled his body. He put his hands to his side, called out to his Adjutant to take his papers, and fell back dead. So ended the career of a gallant gentleman and a brave soldier.

Lieutenant Moffit, the Adjutant, stooped down over the body of his chief, thus exposing himself to the machine-gun fire, and was shot through the head. His death, too, was instantaneous.

We were able to join up with the Green and Purples on our left, but, unfortunately, the battalion of another brigade on our right had failed to gain its objective, and so our right flank, to our detriment, was in the air.

Under most violent counter-attacks we held the line during the night. Our supply of bombs ran out. Captain Arblaster sent several runners back to our old line to ask the O. C. for God's sake to send us more bombs. No bombs were forthcoming, so he rushed back himself through the hell that No Man's Land, then was, made his way through a regular barrage of shell and machine-gun fire, back and then forward again to his company. Our numbers by this time had dwindled down to a mere handful, but still Captain Arblaster and Captain Murray rallied the brave remnant over and over again, and held on like bulldogs. In the early morning, Captain Arblaster, in a hand-to-hand fight with the enemy, was struck down by a Fritz bomb. Captain Murray took charge of the captured position and resisted all attacks. Those who were left realized now that the struggle was hopeless, but they cared not. They looked death in the face without flinching, and resolved to sell their lives dearly.

At 9 a.m. on the 20th, orders were received from our Brigadier-Colonel Pope to retire, and then as we raced back, furiously angry with the dastards who had let us down, hell was let loose. Our retreat was accomplished under a veritable hail of fire of all kinds, our dead littered that field of horror in front of our old line. Those of us who reached that battered trench cared not whether we lived or died. Our soldiers, gaunt, unkempt, and begrimed thanked God silently in their hearts for their lives, then they remembered their pals lying dead out yonder, and they burst into lurid torrents of invective on the Hun, and on the cowards who didn't play the game.

Never shall I forget the scenes of carnage witnessed on that awful night.

The wounded came in or were brought in to the Aid Posts in thousands. The doctors and their A. M. C. dressers had no respite for twenty-four hours. The stretcher-bearers, those greatest heroes of this war, staggered in bearing their maimed and torn burdens. Wearied and spent almost to the end of endurance, they carried on gallantly, went out over and over again into that inferno of blood and fire and death.

Our M. O., Captain Cosgrove, established himself for all time in the respect and love of the men. Gentle as a woman, he spoke cheery words of sympathy and encouragement to our poor lads while he bound their wounds.

The fortitude of the wounded was wonderful.

One lad, Colonel Norris's batman, was badly wounded in the German line. He was told that his Colonel was dead. On hearing the sad news, despite the fact that one leg was all but blown off, and the other badly shattered, he resolved that he would not be a burden to the devoted stretcher-bearers. He crawled back through No Man's Land and eventually reached our lines. He still survives, a maimed victim, and. back in Sydney, remembers as an awful nightmare the shambles of Fromelles.

Another lad, a mere boy, had his nose blown clean away. I remember a wounded officer's words. "For God's sake, let me shake hands with that kid over there." The "kid" was sitting on a bench in the Aid Post waiting patiently until more serious cases were attended to. He was smoking a cigarette and puffed rings of smoke through the bleeding orifices where his nose had been.

Poor old Corporal Duffal, the light-hearted humorist, who used to sing "The Tragedy of a Laundry Woman," "The Face on the Barroom Floor," and other realistic ditties, was brought in very far gone indeed. Even so he would have his joke. The doctor bent down over him: "Well, Duffal, my poor chap, what have they done to you?"

"I'm sure I don't know, Doc. I reckon

they've put me through a bloomin' sausage machine. Anyhow I'm going to prosecute somebody for libel."

"Why, what have they been saying, Duffal ? " "Well, they called that paddock out there No Man's Land. I wasn't there very long when some blinkin' Fritz resented my intrusion, and made a horrible mess of me."

Poor lads, what hearts of gold ! No wonder we read in the papers that Australian troops are very much in evidence when there's anything worth while to be accomplished.

Major Croshaw witnessed more than his share of the horrors of that night. As advance Brigade Major, his work was arduous and extremely perilous. Not once, but many times did he cross the shell-torn field between our front line and the trenches captured by us in the attack. Often he could not get in touch with brigade, but he used his own initiative and carried on. He rallied isolated parties, kept touch with the other brigades of our division, and ultimately advised our B. H. Q. that our withdrawal was imperative, else the remnant of a gallant regiment would be annihilated.

Such was our initiation as a division. Our losses in the advance, during the occupation of the Hun trenches, and in the retreat to our own lines were calamitous. Our battalion fared worse than any other in our brigade, but the others, too, paid heavy toll. Battalions of the other brigades were all but annihilated. Everywhere there was the same fierce resentment against the English divisions who failed to assist us in the affair, and so allowed us to attempt the impossible and be wiped out in the gallant endeavour.

At noon on the 20th, we moved out to a farm near Bac St Maur. The day was bright and warm. A hot meal was provided for the men who, tired and dispirited, lolled about on the grass.

Major Croshaw called the muster roll at 3 p.m. Never shall we forget that sad roll-call. All that was left of us was 150 men and five officers, including the M. O., and the chaplain. Of these five, Captain Thompson and Lieutenant Lovatt were wounded, and had to be evacuated to hospital soon after.

The officers killed in the stunt were Colonel Norris, Major Sampson, gallant Captain Charlie Arblaster (at the mention of whose name even now our men salute and give earnest tribute to an ungazetted hero and V.C.), Captain Harry Pauline, Lieutenants Moffit, Noble, Nelson, Mudge, Pratt, Allan, Rickards and Collier.

Our wounded were Captain Thompson, Lieuts. Evers, Johnson, Smith, Lovatt, Jackson, Francis, Payne, Robertson and Thompson.

Captain Ranson and Lieutenant Bowman were taken prisoners.

We, the survivors, the broken and nerve-shattered remnant of a fine regiment, failed to see the meaning of the task allotted to us at Fromelles. It was hopeless from the very outset. We fought as gallant Anzacs always do, though this time against overwhelming odds. The soldiers of our division attempted the impossible with an intrepidity unsurpassed in the annals of British warfare. Later on we were told that our High Command foresaw the result exactly as it occurred, but it was intended to use us as a holocaust for the salvation of other divisions then hard pressed in another part of the line. A fine compliment, forsooth! It cost us the blood of our bravest and best.

This was the battle of Fromelles. The casualties to our division alone numbered roughly 7,000, and weren't we flattered when it was alluded to a few days later in the English papers as a *raid* by Australian troops ! ! !

The honours awarded to our battalion for gallantry in this so-called raid were as follows: Major Croshaw and Father Kennedy gained the D.S.O., Captain Cosgrove, Captain Murray, Lieuts. Lovatt, Jackson, and Francis the M.C., Sergeants Myers and Saunders, the D.C.M., Privates Devery and Sowton, the Military Medal.

SECTION VI

After Fromelles, Major Croshaw was appointed C. O. of the Green and Blacks. Oswald realized what arduous work his promotion entailed. He had to re-constitute from the remnant of the old battalion and from reinforcements a new fighting regiment. But it was work he relished. His wonderful organizing powers now obtained full scope, his energy was indefatigable, his personality made itself felt and the result was, after a few months, a magnifient unit comprised of splendidly-trained officers and men, who took a soldierly pride in their battalion, and were eager to find opportunities to gain for it further renown and glory.

I have rarely met men of such charm of manner as Colonel Croshaw possessed. He could be brusque and harsh with people whom he deemed rotters. On parade he was strict and soldierly but never over-bearing. At mess he was an English gentleman, always courteous, a delightful host, a brilliant conversationalist, with a keen appreciation of humour, quick at repartee, a lover of music and song, always assiduous in his endeavours to make the mess-room a bright cheery place—the convivial rendezvous of his officers, who under him were always a united and happy fraternity.

General McKay was evidently unable to secure a long respite from the trenches for his division. On the 22nd of July, we moved forward to our old positions at Fleurbaix. Captain Cosgrove and I bade " Au Revoir " to the kindly people in whose home in Bac St Maur we had enjoyed a much-appreciated rest after the horrors of Fromelles. Monsieur, our host, invited us to dinner next day, his invitation was volubly supported by Mesdames, his mother and wife. They explained that they would prepare a veritable banquet for us, the " pièce de resistance " of the feast was to be " Une tête de veau." We promised we would come if it were at all possible, but, unfortunately, we were unable to attend and do justice to Mesdames' cuisine.

We went into our old positions at Fleurbaix. The fine house which had been our battalion headquarters before was as we left it, so we resumed our occupation of it and were tolerably comfortable.

Lieutenant Moysey-Adams, who had been evacuated to hospital on our arrival in France, reported back again, and was appointed Adjutant. Captain Vine-Hall, who had been at Esterres for some weeks as Town Major, resumed real soldiering with us. Lieutenants Robertson and Thompson, who had been slightly wounded, and had rested for some days at the Field Ambulance, also returned to duty. Another officer, Lieutenant Smythe, arr ved from Etaples. Our reinforcements arrived each day in good muster. On the 24th of July, six officers and one hundred and ninety-four men of the Fourth Light Horse were attached for duty. They were under Major Armstrong, an officer who endeared himself to all of us by his breezy geniality and imperturable good humour.

On the morning after our return to Fleurbaix, I was roused from sleep by a loud explosion. A few minutes later an orderly came rushing upstairs and asked for the doctor. I hastened down with Captain Cosgrove, crossed the street to the Mairie right opposite our billet. The enemy had fired five shells into the building itself. Reinforcements had arrived for us about midnight and were quartered in the place. Three were killed and three were badly wounded. Two of these died in the Ambulance Car. It was a horrible affair, and a rude welcome for those poor lads fresh from Australia.

For the next few days life was pleasant enough. The weather was warm and bright, so we moved about a good deal. There were many civilians still in the town—mostly women and old grandfathers. It was certainly evident that not a few of the Froggies who lived here were not too kindly disposed towards us. In unguarded moments they openly expressed their sympathy with, and their admiration for the Hun. There were some incidents which we laugh at now when we recall them.

Colonel Croshaw asked us at mess one evening if we had noticed the movements and evolutions of a certain white horse. We hadn't observed.

"Well," said the Colonel, "the people next door—two evil-looking harridans and their very Hunish-looking brother—run an estaminet. I have heard from some of these men that they are not at all sympathetic or kindly disposed towards us. Moreover, they own this mysterious white horse. I have had my eye on the blasted steed, and have noticed that he is moved about to different fields every evening and removed early next morning. It can't be a coincidence that Fritz invariably shells some time during the day the place where the white nag was the evening before. You know Fritz planes are over every evening and morning, so it looks jolly certain that the owner of the cursed horse is a spy, and is using the charger to our detriment."

"How about seizing the immaculate Rosinante?" the doctor queried.

"An excellent suggestion, Doc.! Moysey, will you send for Jennings and instruct him to detail an N. C. O. and four men to bring that white horse up here, and shove it into the stable near the A. M. C. billet, under guard."

"Very well, Sir," Moysey-Adams replied. He saluted, and went out to issue instructions to the R. S. M.

A quarter of an hour later, a messenger reported that reinforcements were necessary, as the two viragoes from next door had gone to the rescue of their snow-white steed, and were engaged in fierce conflict with the party detailed by the R. S. M.

We all hurried to the fray. The Corporal in charge of the party was hanging on to the horse's head. One man was struggling with the stolid-faced brother. The other three were trying to keep back the infuriated spinster sisters, who screamed, and scratched, and clawed, to the detriment of our Anzac's facial beauty. Our lads disdained to strike or even push the Furies. In the greatest confusion they tried to keep them off, and in good Australian vernacular told the Amazons their pedigree, while hundreds of Billjims laughed in wild appreciation of the joke. If our boys spoke correctly the hags were scarcely thoroughbred ladies.

The Colonel laughed himself hoarse ; so did we. At last the doctor went to the rescue. He explained in very polite French to the frenized women that they and the horse were suspects, that their resistance was futile, that the charger would be well treated though interned, that they would likewise be clinked if they didn't behave, that their estaminet would be placed permanently " out of bounds " to the soldiers, and many other threats. His intervention had the desired effect. The horse was escorted to durance vile, we followed the procession. Those devil's daughters walked in our wake and cursed us in the vilest vocabulary their Franco-Flemish dialect owned.

The milk-white steed remained under guard several days during which period there was no more suspicious shelling of batteries and billets.

A week or so later I made an ass of myself in my zeal to catch a real live spy.

On several occasions my batman and I had noticed a suspicious, bullet-headed, villainous, Hunnish-looking fellow crossing the fields in the neighbourhood. He passed by my window one afternoon (when I lived in a wooden hut near the farm, called Port-a-Clou). He was decidedly an ugly and sinster-looking fellow.

He wore a bandage over his right eye and a battered hat was pulled down over his brows. I thought it strange that he should always avoid the roads and pursue his mysterious errands across the fields. I immediately decided to arrest him.

"Here, Dick," I exclaimed to my trusty follower. "See, there's that bloke we've noticed slouching round the place the other day. Get after him and bring him back here, by force, if necessary."

Dick bolted off like a greyhound, and called out "Halt." The fellow hastened his pace. Dick cried out "Arretez." His stentorian command was but an incentive to speed on the other's part. Dick rushed at him, tripped him up "toute de suite," took him by the back of the neck, shook him, caressed the back of his trousers with his boot, and pushed him before him back to me. Meantime the doctor had arrived on the scene.

The wretched prisoner trembled like a frightened rat. I questioned him sternly, as to who he was and what he was doing round these parts.

He bleated in reply, "Mais, Monsieur, pourquoi? Je suis le facteur." I nearly took a fit. We had arrested the village postman. To prove his statement, he opened the bag he carried on his shoulder, and displayed a bundle of letters. I pointed to the door and told him clear. I buried my hands in my pockets and exclaimed, "Well, I'll be jiggered." The doctor and Dick rolled over on the grass in convulsions of laughter. Well, I laughed too, but that evening at mess, and many evenings afterwards, that blessed doctor entertained the C. O. and officers with a very much exaggerated account of my spy-capture.

Exactly a week after our return to Fleurbaix we had rather an exciting experience.

According to our usual custom, Captain Cosgrove and I came up to our rooms after lunch to enjoy a siesta for an hour. I was asleep about ten minutes when I heard first the shriek and then the crash of two enemy shells in quick succession. I had grown accustomed to the flight of those deadly missiles over my abode, and so this time I turned over and resolved to sleep on. My intentions were frustrated. Colonel Croshaw came into my room.

"I say, K———, old chap. Come out of here immediately. I have already warned Cosgrove and everybody else. Those shells have landed in the garden. I am convinced Fritz has the range of this place and will get it to-day. I have ordered the men in billets to get out to those trenches in the field near by. We, the Headquarters people, must find shelter in that emergency dug-out at the back of the house."

I put on my tunic and hat, and followed the C. O. downstairs. We had arrived at the last step when there was a terrific crash. A shell had cut clean through the roof, and exploded in my room. The house shook, and we thought it was going to topple over on us. The glass roof of the dining-room shivered and smashed on to the floor. There was a shower of plaster, broken bricks, and other *débris* all round us, but not a single fragment touched us. Every one had got clear except a signaller who was slightly wounded. We all took refuge in our funk-hole, and remained imprisoned there with only short intervals between shell-bursts, when we came up to investigate the damage.

Two more shells hit the doomed house, and made of it a veritable ruin. Several shells burst close by in the garden. Fortunately our flimsy sand-bag shelter escaped. Just as well for us as it was scarcely bomb-proof.

The bombardment lasted from 2 p.m. to 6.30 p.m. At 6 p.m. the poor old church was on fire, several buildings near by were also in flames. We marched out of the martyred town at 11.30 p.m. to billets near by. The flames of the burning church and the houses round about lit up the streets with weird effect, and caused us to appear a grotesque army of phantoms as we moved out. Our new Brigadier—General Hobkirk—had arranged our occupation of Port-à-Clou farm just outside the town. C and D companies took shelter in the school buildings away from the shelled area. We turned in about 1 a.m. The last words I heard Cosgrove say were, "Well, it would be rather a stretch of imagination to describe this life as restful."

SECTION VII.

During the next six weeks we learned to regard the Fleurbaix sector as a sort of home. The routine arrangements for our brigade were two battalions in the front line at a time, the other two being in reserve at Fleurbaix. The period in the front line was a fortnight, which was followed by a fortnight in billets at and near Port-à-Clou.

There were usually casualties on the evening of our going into the line, and also when coming out. Now and again, while in the front trenches, Fritz shelled us rather heavily, so that it was an exceptionally lucky day when we did not have at least two or three casualties.

When our battalion was in the line, our

battalion headquarters were near a ruined brick house, called Foray Farm. Here we lived in dug-outs. By day the place was quiet enough, but from dusk onwards it was an unhealthy spot, and one had to keep close to the sand-bags and keep one's head down, in order to dodge the hissing machine-gun and rifle bullets.

The quasi-dug-out in which the doctor and I lived was shrapnel proof, nothing more. How I hated the musty, stifling atmosphere of that dug-out. A sand-bag partition divided it into compartments. Captain Cosgrove had two medical stretchers put in. We fixed these on old cases and made ourselves tolerably comfortable bunks. The sociable M. O. also had a few sand-bags taken out of the partition, and so we could recline on our beds and see one another. We could also carry on a conversation until we felt disposed to sleep. We had to stay in the infernal tomb by night, but during the day we entered it only when necessary. We developed the habit of paying social calls on our friends in the front line. One day we would spend a few hours with A company officers in their dug-out. The next day we would break bread with the genial Steve Armstrong and his dashing Light Horse officers. Then there was Tom Dick's subterranean mansion, the headquarters of the

Brigade Machine-Gun Company, where we were always made heartily welcome by gay Captain Tom and his Lieutenants. And so we whiled away the weary hours, and laughed, and jested as if we were thousands of miles away from the firing line, instead of actually living in the arena of war and death.

The Regimental Aid Post was about two hundred yards distant from our rat-infested catacomb. Here the brave and devoted Corporal Jimmy Harrop, with his team of A. M. C. dressers, lived. Often Cosgrove and I were roused by night to attend to a wounded soldier at the Aid Post. To me it used to seem like a fantastic dream, the midnight hurried walk up the sap along the duck-boards, while the guns roared, the flares flung up in the air cast phantom lights, and the bullets pinged and hissed over our heads.

I remember one night particularly. The enemy shelled the road and the sap near our residence. For three hours without a break he raised hell all round us with H. E. and shrapnel. Before the deadly racket commenced, I had turned in and dosed off to sleep. Cosgrove awakened me.

"I say, friend," he said solemnly, "make ready, for to-night we die. They have been smashing things up all round us. If a shell only kisses the damned hole, it will collapse.

My greatest trouble is I have a bottle of precious Johnny Walker, black label, here. 'Twill be a darned shame if it is lost. What do you say to our drinking it lest it may be wasted ?"

'Twas always thus with dear old Cossy. He could jest and be facetious even when the skeleton monster, Death, brandished his scythe to slay.

Every day we received some evidence of Colonel Croshaw's abilities as a Commanding Officer. The man was a marvel. Nobody knew when he was likely to appear at any of the posts occupied by our people. The fact that he had been in the front line in the morning was no guarantee that he would not visit there in the evening. Our transport people, too, realized that though well back and enjoying comparative comfort, they were not forgotten by the C. O. When we first went into the line from Port-à-Clou, they took things rather easy. The Colonel paid them an unexpected call early one morning. Well, those complacent muleteers got the shock of their lives. They received such a straffing that they averred a bombardment was mild in comparison. The transport camp was a regular hive of industry and activity after that memorable shaking-up.

When out at Port-à-Clou, all ranks had an

enjoyable time. The billets, taking into consideration our proximity to the line, were good. Officers and men obtained liberal leave, and we varied the monotony of military life with occasional trips to Esterre, Armentières, Steenwark, and other adjacent towns. After a term in the trenches the very fact of sitting down to lunch or tea at damask-covered and silver-equipped tables in snug little restaurants in these places was a pleasure in itself.

Indeed, our headquarters mess was all that could be desired. Our carterer, Gallagher, was priceless. We realized this so thoroughly that we were always inviting officers to dinner in order to show them how we did ourselves. Those were pleasant days, and we were light-hearted men who adopted the philosophy of taking every day as it came and trusting to God for the morrow.

On the 2nd of September, to our great regret, Major Armstrong and his Light Horse officers and men who had been attached to us since Fromelles, left us to rejoin their own unit. Three of their N. C. O's had applied for infantry commissions in our battalion. The commissions were granted, and so we acquired three of our bravest and most gallant subs.—Lieutenants Cooper, Waite, and Hill.

About this time, too, Captain Ramsay, M.C.,

rejoined us. He had been evacuated to hospital in Egypt. Bob Ramsay was perhaps the most talented officer in the old regiment. He was certainly the most interesting problem in contradictions I've tried to solve.

Had Bob Ramsay, when younger, adopted soldering as a profession, had he in addition been possessed of the advantages that a liberal education bestows, I am quite sure that his military career would have been exceptionally brilliant. Even as things were, with only an ordinary education but with considerable natural ability, he was a company commander who would make his mark in any regiment. At any rate he was an asset to us. In the line he thought of nothing else but his job. Out of the line he was the most rollicking and apparently the most irresponsible officer in the battalion. Nevertheless he was never absent from morning parade, and always appeared trim and soldierly. His laugh was a speciality, and so was his gift of winning men's affection. Captain Bob, as the men called him, could lead the way to the most dare-devil and hazardous stunt, and there was not one officer, N. C. O., or private, who wouldn't follow him.

Colonel Croshaw once said of him : " Ramsay is a devil, but if hell were peopled with deils of his ilk, I should ask for bi-annual leave there from the other place."

Whereupon somebody answered: "Faith, Sir, you may command a division down there and that would be a hell of a job, for they tell us there's no getting out of the show."

On the 7th of September, our battalion marched to La Motte where we were to undergo special training in wood-fighting. This was the alleged reason for the move. In reality a very fine compliment was paid us. We were singled out by the division as the battalion that had shown the greatest gallantry and consequently had suffered the most at Fromelles. The wood-fighting training would not occupy very much time each day, and therefore our ten days at La Motte would be an excellent opportunity to give us a complete rest away from the sound of the guns. It would also give us a chance to re-organize.

La Motte will always be associated in our minds with many comical incidents.

We were camped near a grand old wood not very far from Hazebrouck. The Colonel lived in the house near by where our headquarters mess was arranged. Three Imperial officers messed with us. They were entirely different types.

One was an exquisite creature—a Major. His complexion was strawberry and cream. His clothes were the acme of Bond Street art. His accent was the most remarkable of English affectations in the mispronunciation of English. He was a most superb ass, God bless him. He used to talk of " bawages " and " twenches " and you funny Austwalians I simply love you, don't cher know. You are so awfully " je ne sais quoi " don't che know. Well, so awfully bloody."

Oh dear, he was the softest thing in uniform.

What fantastic exaggerations of Australian life and customs we used to dish up for him, and the innocent opened his mouth in amazement and swallowed them all.

Captains Pearson and Cosgrove used to discourse for his edification of their black wives in Australia, servants to their lawful wives. They used to speak of their scores of quadroon children, and pretend to converse in the native Australian aboriginal language by stringing out a chain of native names.

Pearson would roll his eyes and distort his face and address the Doctor thus:

"Bobinawarrah, Eupotypotpon, Carragamungee!"

The doctor would make still more violent contortions, and reply:

"Yarrawonga, Wangaratta, Jerilderee, Boorhamon!"

Meantime, Colonel Croshaw and the others were on the verge of apoplexy in the endeavour to keep serious.

The other Major was a dear old Scotchman, whose accent was as pleasant as a draught of Johnny Walker's extra special. He had the driest humour and the quaintest expressions, and always concluded his many yarns with "Mind ye the noo, it's a fact I'm telling ye."

The third Imperial officer who messed with us during our stay at La Motte was that type of Englishman to whom I always yield admiration and respect. He was courteous and broad-minded. He had travelled much, and was an excellent raconteur. He spoke without affectation, and though an officer who had served with distinction in India, and in France in the early days of this war, was very modest when induced at all to talk of his own experiences.

The afternoons at La Motte were generally free. The Colonel allowed a percentage of the officers leave to Hazebrouck. Some of the officers enjoyed themselves with a vengence. Captain Ramsay particularly made the most of those festive hours.

One afternoon, ten officers of the Green and Blacks wended their way to Hazebrouck. They whiled away the hours before dinner each according to his bent. They met by appointment at Les Trois Chateaux and had a right jolly meal. At a table adjacent to theirs a party of prosperous-looking French profiteers made merry. Their remarks were audible, and were resented by several of our subs who spoke French very well. Norman Lovatt informed Bob Bamsay of the uncomplimentary remarks passed by the Froggies at the expense of the redoubtable Captain and his party. Then the fun commenced.

"Excuse me a moment, Gentlemen." Captain Bob apologised to his friends.

He sauntered over to the table where the Frenchies waxed facetious over their Clicquot.

"Pardon me, Messieurs," he exclaimed ultra politely, as he pulled a chair towards their table and sat down next the most arrogant and raucous of the group. "May I join your merry party?"

"Mais oui Monsieur. You will dreenk with us," replied the fat and prosperous-looking Frenchman at the head of the table. He was evidently the host and the others were his guests.

He filled a glass and held it to Ramsay's lips. The Captain thanked him and proceeded to drink the health of the party, but Monsieur persisted in forcing the wine and so spilt the foaming beverage over Bob's tunic.

The other members of the party thought this a great joke and laughed hilariously, but Captain Ramsay's turn was coming.

He called for another bottle of wine.

"Now gentlemen," he exclaimed, "you will drink with me. I wish you to do so in Australian fashion. We shall begin with my fat friend here whose manners are so charming."

Bob seized the bottle. With his left hand he grabbed the Frenchman's nose, tilted his head and poured the wine down his throat. The Froggie spluttered and choked, but Ramsay did not desist until he had almost smothered him. Then things happened. The other profiteers rushed to the rescue of their host, and gesticulated and chattered and screamed as only excited Frenchmen can. But the Captain's friends now took part in the fun. The room was a Bedlam in five minutes. Madame called the gendarmes. These, assisted by the whole staff of the estaminet, finally succeeded in ejecting the laughing Australians, but not before they had tweaked the noses of their antagonists to some effect. Before they departed they won over Madame by paying liberally for the damage to her glass-ware and crockery.

While at La Motte Major Higgins and Captain Roberts, who had been transferred to the Training Battalion in Egypt, rejoined us. About this time, too, Lieutenants Johnson and Lang returned quite hale and hearty again.

We marched back from La Motte to Fleurbaix on the 18th of September. From the 21st to October the 8th, we were in the front line. On the 13th of October our whole division moved *en route* for the Somme.

SECTION VIII.

When we left the Fleurbaix sector, we had only a very vague idea regarding our destination. Various wild rumours, "Furphys," as the men styled them, were current. We soon discovered that we were bound for the Somme area, and were to join with other divisions in a grand offensive. An order was issued that only what was absolutely necessary in the shape of kit was to be taken, the residue was to be stored at Sailly under guard.

We travelled on motor-lorries to our new billets near the village of Outterstene. Here we remained until the 16th. It was a treat, this short sojourn in a charming country district away from the din and traffic, and the crude, stern realities of the forward area. All of us, officers and men, realizing that there was another sharp ordeal ahead of us, forgot our cares and worries, and made the most of those Arcadian days. In the farm where the headquarters officers were billeted there were three very charming madamoiselles. One of these related to us one morning that an amorous officer serenaded her window for a few hours the previous night. She enjoyed playing Juliet to his Romeo, but when he ventured to scale my lady's bower she threw a bucket of cold water over him and so cooled his ardour. The only clue she could give us as to his identity was that he wore spurs. Consequently, a certain gay gallant who invariably went about be-spurred was suspect and chaffed unmercifully.

All good things come to an end, so did our stay at Outterstene. We marched out on the night of the 16th, and entrained near Baileul at 2 a.m. on the 17th of October, but the train did not move out of the station until 5.30 a.m. We passed through Saint Omer, Calais, Boulogne, Etaples, Abbeyville and arrived at our destination, Pont Remy, at 4 p.m. We marched about 2½ miles to Vauchelles, where we were very comfortably billeted. The headquarters officers were housed in a charming chateau, whose proprietor—the Baron de Rocquigny—still lived there with a small retinue of servants. All his sons were away at the front, and all his daughters were married or had taken the veil. Of sons and daughters this polite but penurious old patriarch had been responsible for twenty-four.

We were allotted very comfortable rooms. Mine, I believe, was the nursery. On shelves all round the walls were ranged antediluvian toys and much-abused dolls. The bed was most comfortable, indeed it was a luxury to sleep between fragrant sheets again.

Vauchelles was only a few miles from Abbeville, one of the cleanest and most up-to-date French country towns I've been in. On the evening of the 18th a few of us walked to Abbeville and explored the place. The old abbey was well worth a visit, so was the excellent hotel where we dined " à la carte " and were well catered for.

On the 20th of October, we marched out of Vauchelles at 4.30 a.m. The morning was cold and wet, the march long, and all of us ravenously hungry. No arrangements had been made for feeding the men. They were ordéred to carry their emergency rations which, of course, they were forbidden to use.

We halted an hour at the brigade assembly ground. Then we got on board a long line of French motor lorries and travelled about twenty miles on them. A French officer was in charge of each lot of twenty lorries. These officers had motor-cars at their disposal, and were able to find room in them for most of the officers of our brigade. Lieutenant Sweetnam and I were fortunate enough to find two available seats in a Daimler car. The French captain, whose property it was, treated us very courteously. He carried a plentiful supply of excellent cognac which he insisted on our sampling. We ran through Amiens, at which city we were barely able to have a passing glimpse. Our lorries halted some miles out of Meaulte, so we had to march from there to our destination.

Colonel Croshaw, with the other Battalion Commanders, had gone on ahead two days before to inspect the part of the line we were to take over. As for us, we had no idea we were going right forward that evening. We thought we would be billeted in or near Meaulte for a day at least, but we were destined to disappointment.

In Meaulte we were held up for an hour owing to the congestion of traffic in the narrow village street. Again we moved off.

To our consternation, we were marched right up to the Somme battlefield. While it was daylight we beheld vestiges of those villages recently captured from the Germans. Literally, not a stone was left on a stone, only the cellars were left.

It was a weird, wild, desolate scene. The

guns blazed away. Flares lit up the war-scarred landscape. Night came on, a cold drizzle set in, and still on we marched, tired, hungry and dispirited. At last we stumbled off the road into a muddy field called Pommières Redoubt. Here the greatest confusion prevailed. In the darkness officers found it difficult to muster their men. There was no shelter, no cover for the poor unfortunate men. Most of us spent the night in the open under drizzling rain. We had no blankets, no anything, as the transport had not yet arrived. Captain Murray and Lieutenant Lang discovered an abandoned tent which they erected. Jack Murray sent his batman to find me and invite me to share this tent with him and his company officers. I hastened to avail myself of this protection from the rain. We sat round and smoked and yarned until, despite wet clothes and the damp floor on which we sprawled, we slept fitfully for a few hours. Towards morning a hard frost set in. As soon as it was dawn, we got out and moved about in order to restore circulation and thaw our frozen limbs. Long before breakfast was available, Bluey Ward, who was always eager to do favours to others, brought me a steaming cup of hot cocoa and saved my life.

The transport had arrived during the night;

the cookers were soon negotiated by the
" bablin' brooks," a hot breakfast was served
and appreciated by all of us. After we had
swallowed it, we viewed the situation with a
more hopeful outlook.

On the 21st October Colonel Croshaw took
six hundred men and most of the officers into
the line. Major Higgins, with Mr. Jennings
as Adjutant to him, took charge of the détails
at an improvised camp near Pommières
Redoubt.

The trenches were frightful. During the
seven days of our stay in the lines there
was continuous rain. The winter had set
in with a vengeance. The front line was
merely a series of connected shell-holes in
which the men were knee deep in half-frozen
mud and slush. The approaches and communication saps were mud canals actually.
Rather than risk immersion to the chin in
them, we preferred to walk along in the open
under the enemy fire.

We remained in the line until the 28th.
Part of the time we occupied the support
trenches, the remainder we spent in the
front line. The suffering endured by the men
from frozen feet and all the other awful conditions was acute, but they bore up like
heroes. Each day we paid our toll in casualties. Sometimes the enemy put regular

barrages of shell-fire into our lines, to which our guns replied with double intensity.

Incessant rain rendered the projected offensive impossible, at least for the time being. At last we were relieved, and dragged our weary limbs out of that foul quagmire of horror and death. Officers and men alike had reached the limit of endurance. Unkempt, unshaven, our clothes caked with mud, we waded back through those awful communication saps, and after night had fallen arrived at our camp. Oswald Croshaw was well-nigh exhausted, but even so, he was so zealous for the men's comfort that he would not enjoy rest or refreshment until he had satisfied himself that all his men had been made tolerably comfortable.

Our spell out of the line was only of a very short duration. We marched in again on the 31st and endured the same privations as before until the 5th of November. The weather brightened up on the last two days before we were relieved, and though a month of dry weather could scarce improve the conditions under foot, still it was some assuagement of our sufferings to see blue skies above us, and to dry our sodden garments in the warm sunshine.

On the 5th of November we marched out to billets in Ribmont. On the 8th we marched further back still to very much more comfortable quarters at Coisy, a village about six miles distant from Amiens. While here, Colonel Croshaw went to England on leave. Major Higgins took command of the battalion during his absence.

The Colonel had more than earned his furlough. He was as eager and buoyant as a schoolboy bound for home at the end of a long college term. On the evening before his departure we gave him a dinner which was indeed a breezy function. His only regret was that he could not take all of us fellows with him, but our time was coming.

Amiens! We all have reminiscences of this historic French city. These memories for some Australians are not of the most satisfactory kind. Many fellows fresh from the trenches, inspired by that mad irresponsibility that preludes recklessness and develops into licence, have good reason to curse Amiens. Some of us kindred spirits of the Green and Blacks look back on some right festive and merry evenings spent there. We enjoyed ourselves to our heart's content, but our visits left no qualms of conscience, for we always avoided excess.

Major Higgins and Captain Cosgrove dined one evening at Amiens with two French officers. They had come in on a motor lorry and trusted to luck for a ride home, but they had not reckoned on a sumptuous repast nor its inevitable aftermath. Eventually they linked arms in a most loving manner and proceeded to walk home. The first mile was fatal to their complacency and their admiration for one another. They came to the cross-roads and weren't sure which turn to take. They differed, and the argument became rather verbose and slightly personal. Anyhow the M.O. felt in good form. He hailed the Major as a fat old ——— (you won't find the word in your dictionary), and asked him to hop out. The Major had a good sense of humour. He laughed heartily at the pugilistic son of Esculapius. His laughter quelled the doctor's wrath. They agreed that they were a pair of blithering idiots, padded the hoof again, and arrived home so sanely sober that they were able to appreciate a whiskey before they turned in.

Our good time at Coissy ended on the 19th November. We marched out at 6.30 a.m. Motor lorries conveyed us to Buire, a wretched village where our billets were filthy hovels.

The people here were mercenary and unscrupulous. They would sell their souls for money. Their women-folk had long ago bartered their virtue and had battened on regiment after regiment of British troops since the war commenced.

Conditions generally were satisfactory for us. We were scattered in a bewildering fashion. The M.O., the Q.M., and other officers who had to move about and visit the different companies swore more than they had ever done when the battalion was in the line. Major Thompson's company was fully five miles away engaged on fatigue work at Vivier Mills. Captain Roberts had to take his men to Meaulte for similar duties. One of his platoons was ordered to the M.M. Dump near Albert. Headquarters and the other companies were stabled at Buire.

We remained posted thus three days. Had we been detained longer the Q.M., and an appreciable number of other people would have qualified for the mad-house.

SECTION IX.

On the 21st November we marched out in the early morning from Buire. Our destination was Mametz Camp. This place was most decidedly uninviting. The camp consisted of elephant huts erected on piles on a sea of mud. The approaches were awful, and the huts themselves were left in a most filthy condition by the troops we had relieved.

The weather now was bitterly cold. During our four days stay at Mametz our men were constantly requisitioned for fatigue work on the neighbouring roads and railway lines. It was pitiable to see them return each evening to their inhospitable camp. Tired, and half-frozen, they had to wade knee-deep in mud, in order to reach their huts from the main road.

We moved again on the 25th to a camp further forward. Mametz was bad. Montauban was a thousand times worse. Fortunately Colonel Croshaw returned from leave on the evening of our arrival there.

Next morning he asked me to go round the camp with him. We donned rubber boots that reached to our hips, armed ourselves with stout walking-sticks, and set out. There was a duck-board track running along the front of the huts, but this was out of repair and was broken in several places. Right in front of the hut occupied by the Headquarters officers there was an odoriferous shell-hole, five or six feet deep and some twenty feet in circumference. This hole was filled with water. In it floated refuse of all kinds. A limber had bogged there the night before and was still there half submerged. The exit from the camp was a track over half-a-mile in length buried under three feet of liquid mud.

"Damn those engineers!" the Colonel exclaimed. "They haven't done a darned thing to this place for months. It's merely a matter of drainage. This place is waterlogged and will be uninhabitable after the next heavy rainfall. Why, this track is positively perilous. It is as easy as sin to wander off it by night and be drowned in one of those cursed shell-holes hidden 'neath the mud. By all accounts we are going to be here some weeks. Come, let's get back. I shall order my horse and ride over to the C. R. E. Headquarters. How the devil are we going to avoid evacuations from trench-feet if the men have to wallow in this foul filth?"

With his characteristic energy Colonel Croshaw rode off. He interviewed the Colonel of the Engineers, told him some breezy truths that spoiled that rotund officer's appetite for his luncheon. From there our C.O. rode to divisional headquarters. He used his sarcasm to some effect when he compared our pestiferous camp with their snug and sumptuous quarters. At any rate he woke them up. That evening we were visited by several very irate and red-tabbed staff people. The Colonel led them round the camp by the filthiest route. Their visit ended, he came back to us well pleased with his day's work, and chuckling at the muddy discomfiture of the glorified divisional visitors.

Two days later there there was a noticeable improvement in the camp and its approaches.

Our stay at Montauban lasted a fortnight. During that time we were Corps troops and our men were employed on fatigues at the rail-head and elsewhere. Shells burst near our camp every evening, but we escaped. On the 4th of December the rail-head was shelled. Two of our men were killed and two wounded.

Despite cold, inclement weather and miserable surroundings, we had some merry evenings at Montauban. Owing to the Colonel's exertions, the men were carefully housed and well fed with wholesome hot stews and soups. One hut was set apart as a drying shed. In it several glowing braziers were kept going. The men's wet socks were hung up and dried there, so that each evening, on their return from work, there was a dry change of foot-wear for them.

In the headquarters officers' hut we were rather congested but tolerably comfortable. There were the Colonel, Major Higgins, Doctor Cosgrove and I, Captain Pearson, Captain Geof. Street, the Brigade Staff Captain, who lived with us, Lieutenants Moysey-Adams and Jennings, the Adjutant and Assistant-Adjutant. For the first two nights after our arrival we rolled our valises out on the muddy floor, tied ourselves into our sleeping-bags, and, despite the cold and discomfort, slept tolerably well. But we were much better off during the remainder of our stay. Our batmen got busy and made us stretchers from wood and wire netting. No downy beds in luxurious hotels ever seemed so comfortable or were more appreciated by us than these rickety ramshackle couches.

There were many comical and ludicrous incidents during our stay at Montauban.

On the evening of our arrival we were all very much out of sorts. Cold and exhausted, dripping wet and mud-begrimed, we stumbled into the huts allotted to us. The reader can therefore realize how badly disposed we were to brook insolence from a cheeky officer's servant. When we entered our inhospitable shack we found a batman in possession. He coolly informed us that his boss was a lieutenant whose regiment was in the line, that the said lieutenant was suffering from shell-shock and was detailed to remain behind and occupy this shed as a refuge for other damaged warriors, that, therefore, we were in the wrong box and had better trek.

Captain Cosgrove yawned and told the bumptious batman that we were really too tired to enjoy his little joke, so he had better make himself scarce.

The result was more insolence from the imperturbable Tommy, whereupon Captain Cosgrove dexterously flung a lump of coal at the fellow and followed up the attack with a running kick. The doctor's riding boot arrived with some effect on the batman's subsequent anatomy just as he was speeding out of the door. The kick sped him over more space than he had calculated on. He found himself immersed to his chin in the Eau-de-Cologne reservoir outside the door. The Captain's equilibrium, as well as his equanimity, suffered disturbance. Having inflicted condign punishment on his tormentor, he slipped on the muddy floor, and came down with a crash on the boards. There was much laughter from the onlookers.

Every evening, our day's duty ended and dinner over, we used to sit round the glowing brazier and sing songs and spin yarns. Later we turned in and rolled ourselves up in our blankets. Mr. Jennings used to brew us a steaming mug of rum toddy, this enhanced our comfort and imparted a delightful glow. All the time the guns crashed and shells exploded near our camp, but we trusted to Providence, and slept soundly, near though we were to the firing line.

The Major wasn't a safe person to entrust secrets to. He talked in his sleep and so contributed not a little to our amusement for the first few nights. After that his hallucinations bored us somewhat and his disclosures were summarily interrupted by a shower of tin pannikins and other offensive missiles. The doctor used to draw him out and agree with or contradict him as he felt inclined. the result was ludicrous in the extreme. The Colonel and the rest of us fairly shook with laughter until we grew tired of Percy's ramblings, then we closed the entertainment.

On the 13th of December the battalion marched out from Montauban to Delville Wood Camp. Our fellows named the new camp Devil's Wood." It merited the name. A more sinister and unhealthy spot could scarce be found along the Western battle-line.

On the 16th we moved into the front line. Our details remained at Bernafay Wood. We remained in the line until the 20th. The trenches were knee-deep in semi-frozen mud and slush. The weather was cold, wet, and stormy. Our poor lads suffered terribly owing to the inclement weather conditions, but owing to the Colonel's care for his men, and the assistance given him by all his officers, we had very few cases of trench feet by comparison with other battalions. Our casualties were two killed and two wounded.

On the 20th December we moved from the front line to Camp at Trones Wood. Here reinforcements, comprising one officer and twenty other ranks, marched in. On the 21st we moved from Trones Wood to Adelaide Camp, Montauban. We moved again on the 22nd, journeying by rail from Quarry Siding to Meaulte and marched from there to Buire. Here we remained in billets until January 4th, 1917.

Though the weather during our stay at Buire was generally cold and inclement, we enjoyed ourselves. It was a great boon to be out of the line for Christmas, and we set to work to make it a time of good cheer.

There were several most enjoyable Christmas festivities. The officers gave the men of the battalion a Christmas dinner. This function was indeed a huge success. Captain Bob Ramsay was in charge of the catering, and didn't he scour the country to some effect? We secured a spacious hall for the feast. The walls were festooned with evergreens. The tables groaned 'neath a sumptuous spread. Roast turkey, sucking pigs, hams, sides of beef, and legs of mutton, puddings, trifles, fruit and sweets galore. There was also a plentiful helping of beer and wine, so the men had a right merry Christmas. There was music and song, and of course we had brilliant speeches and felicitations. The lads forgot the privations of the past and the troubles ahead. The keen longings for home and friends were assuaged, and we all looked forward with hope and confidence to the new year.

Colonel Croshaw, with his usual kindness and good-fellowship, gave a dinner to the officers of the battalion. This event will always be remembered by those present as one of the bright spots in the drab monotony and the dark days of blood and death that made up our term of active service. As a host, the Colonel was most courteous and charming. There was no stiffness or forced gaiety. The Colonel was as free with the Junior Sub. as he was with the Second in Command, and so the enjoyment was spontaneous. God knows we did well to abandon ourselves to song and laughter and quaff the sparkling wine-cups heedless of the future, for there were stern and terrible days ahead of us.

A considerable number of reinforcements joined us during our stay at Buire.

On the 4th January, 1917, we marched from Buire to Flesselles *via* Franvilliers. We halted at this latter place and were billeted there that night. Next morning we resumed our march to Flesselles, where we arrived at mid-day. We remained here and enjoyed time for rest and re-organization until the 14th. On the 14th we moved from Flesselles to Buire. On the 16th we moved from Buire to Fricourt Camp, where we remained until the 26th, when we moved forward to Trones Wood. On the 27th January the battalion, minus the details, who moved to Bernafy Wood, moved into the intermediate line. We moved into the front line that night. It was some line, too. As usual we had to pay for the indolence and the inefficiency of the people whom we relieved, and so our lads had to work hard in order to make our sector tenable and habitable. But our men were wonderful, and set to their allotted fatigues with a good humour and determination truly admirable.

Until the end of February we had no respite from line work. The same hopeless trudging in and out from front line to intermediate line, then back to a muddy shell-exposed camp, forward again to the line, and never out of the zone of fire. Moysey-Adams, the Adjutant, broke down under the strain, several other officers were evacuated, but the Colonel still commanded the battalion, and commanded it well. He was indeed a marvel of endurance, a soldier every inch, daily endearing himself more and more to his officers and men by his bravery, and his wonderful consideration for others. Our new Adjutant, Lieutenant Elliott, universally known as Bull, was a very capable young officer. Strong and fearless as a lion, he stood the wear and tear of that trying winter and spring, and became more efficient as the dreary weeks crawled on.

Our casualties were not very numerous during January and February, but there was the inevitable leakage caused by trench feet and trench fever. The others carried on gallantly. They became fatalists in a sense. Their philosophy was, " Let's take every day as it comes! The future is in God's hands."

SECTION X.

The Green and Blacks had long ago earned for themselves a magnificent reputation. In our own division, and right throughout the Australian Army, we were known as the gallant Green and Blacks, and after January, 1917, as Croshaw's Whale Oil Guards. This last name was achieved by us in this manner.

Colonel Croshaw, with the punctilious regard for dress and general turn-out characteristic of the cavalry officer, was always anxious that the men of his battalion should out-rival all others not only by their bravery and efficiency in the line, but by their smartness on parade. Early in January our battalion supplied the Divisional Guards. The Colonel had occasion to visit D. H. Q. one morning. When leaving, he recognised in the sentry one of his own men. He was impressed by the smart and soldierly appearance of the soldier. The fellow's helmet especially attracted his attention. The British trench-helmet, or tin-hat as the Anzacs call it, is not remarkable for its beauty. Usually it is covered with coarse canvas or begrimed with mud. This sentry's helmet was so brightly polished that it shone and glinted in the sunlight. The C.O. questioned him as to his head-gear, but the man seemed abashed and afraid of a reprimand. The Colonel pressed him, and then the resourceful Anzac replied that he had used his ration of whale-oil to burnish his helmet. Instead of a rebuke, the C.O. praised him: "Your turn-out is very creditable. After all, that whale-oil if no good for trench feet is useful for something. I shall see that the whole battalion polish their helmets similarly."

That afternoon the Colonel called a meeting of his officers. Amongst other matters he commented on the smart appearance of the sentry he had spoken to that morning, and instructed his officers to order that all the helmets be treated in the same way. And thus came about our title :—" Croshaw's Whale Oil Guards."

The Whale Oil Guards established their reputation for bravery still more firmly during the next few months.

The enemy, sorely pressed by our terrible artillery, retired to the so-called Hindenburg Line, and so Bapaume and other towns so long coveted by the Allies fell into our hands.

Our routine of duty was much the same as it had been during the month of February. We usually spent about four days at a time in the front line, then were relieved and marched out to the intermediate line for a few days, then back to the advance camps, and the same over again.

During those three months, March, April, and May, Lieutenants Lang, Cooper, Hill, and Jackson, distinguished themselves as officers in charge of patrols and reconnaissance parties in pursuit of the enemy.

On the 14th March, a young and gallant officer, Captain Francis, M.C., was killed. On the same day, in fact by the same shell, was laid low R.S.M. Monro, one of the bravest soldiers in the battalion.

On the 17th March we moved forward, and entered Heaven Trench at 4.15 a.m., just as the enemy was leaving the same trench, and so we established our front line on the old enemy Beaulencourt-Transloy Line.

On the 28th March we moved forward and took up our position as Right Battalion in the Outpost Line.

Colonel Croshaw was appointed O.C. of the Outpost Line, and Major J. J. Murray assumed command of the battalion for the time being.

On the 20th March, one of our bravest officers—Lieutenant Cooper—was killed. His loss cast a gloom over all of us, and more especially over his bosom friends, Lieutenants Billy Waite and Reg. Hill. These two went out to where his body lay, and buried the remains. Peace be to his brave soul.

During March, we had two officers killed, twelve other ranks killed, forty-one other ranks wounded, and four other ranks missing.

On April 1st we were relieved from the Outpost Line by the 31st battalion A.I.F., and proceeded to Velu Wood. The 55th battalion attacked successfully at Doignies. They were reinforced on the 2nd by our B company under Captain Bert Jackson, M.C. This same Captain Jackson was, perhaps, the most popular officer in the battalion. Full of vitality and strong as a lion, he was as honest and straightforward as any man could be. He was a typical Australian, and loved to use Australian slang. He was always bright and cheery, and was known by all of us as Good Old Jacko. Though only twenty-three, he had already been wounded three times. Captain Jackson and his company had a pretty warm time at Doignies, but he brought them through all right.

We were relieved from the front line on the 4th April by the 59th battalion, and returned to Velu Wood and Lebucquire as Right Support Battalion. We were relieved again on the 5th April and marched back to Thilloy on the 6th. On the 20th we marched to Bazentin Camp. On the 21st from Bazentine to Becourt Camp. On the 22nd there was a Brigade Church Parade, attended by the G.O.C. Australian Forces, General Sir William Birdwood. We celebrated Anzac Day on the 25th April by holding Battalion Sports. That evening there was a very enjoyable Brigade Concert. From May 1st to May 6th we enjoyed a much-needed rest. There was, of course, reorganization and training, but we had ample time for sports, football, and athletic competitions of all kinds. The weather conditions were ideal, and the spirits and *morale* of the troops never better.

Our Divisional Commander, Major-General Hobbs, who had succeeded Major-General

McKay, believed in the efficacy of sports and merry-makings. He argued that the lives of the soldiers were generally fraught with so many horrors and hardships that it was necessary to beguile their days out of the line with as much sport and recreation as was compatible.

On the 7th May, at 12.30 a.m., orders were received from Brigade to proceed in eight hours' time to the forward area. We moved out from Becourt at 8 a.m., marched to Albert and entrained on the first train to Bapaume with Brigade Headquarters, and the 56th battalion. In accordance with instructions, we left at Becourt 6 officers and 160 other ranks. The strength of the battalion as it moved forward was 21 officers and 660 other ranks. The C. O., Colonel Croshaw, was unable to go forward owing to an accident while riding at the Divisional Horse Show some days before. Major Thompson, M.C., took command of the battalion for the time being. We detrained at Bapaume at 1 p.m. on the 7th, and marched to the Reserve Line (Beugny-Ytres). Here we occupied the trench system forward of Beugnatre.

On the 8th, the battalion moved forward at night through Vaula and Noreuil to the front line, where we relieved the 10th and 12th battalions A.I.F. The sector taken over was the ridge in the Hindenburg Line at Bullecourt, and immediately in front of Riencourt-Les-Carnicourt. The line on the whole was fairly good. During our five days' occupation of it the shelling was terrific. The enemy bombarded us incessantly. Among the projectiles were many gas-shells.

On the 9th, Lieutenant A. O. Corry was wounded. Three other ranks were killed, and twenty-six other ranks were wounded.

On the 10th May, Lieutenant J. M. Jefferson was killed, Lieutenant Reg. Hill was wounded. One other rank was killed and thirteen other ranks were wounded. Information was received that the enemy was massing troops for an attack. Our artillery shelled them heavily so the attack did not eventuate.

During the 11th and 12th of May the enemy artillery was very active. We had a considerable number of casualties from shellfire. The weather had become very warm, and the stench from the vast number of unburied corpses lying about was so revolting that it was almost unbearable.

We were relieved by the 54th battalion on the night of the 13th. The relief was completed by 2.15 a.m. on the 14th. During the night we had four men killed and twenty-six wounded. The battalion moved into the support line near Noreuil. Colonel Croshaw took over command from Major Thompson on the night of the 13th. During the time spent by us in the support lines the enemy shelling, though still considerable, was much less active. The men were occupied in carrying perquisites to the front line and working on the new dug-outs in the support lines. There was a very heavy gas-shell bombardment on the night of the 14th. We had two casualties.

On the 18th May Colonel Croshaw was wounded. About 5 p.m. a party was moving along the sunken road near Battalion Headquarters, when they suddenly came under very heavy shell-fire. Colonel Croshaw, regardless of his own safety, went out into the road. He was giving instructions for the protection of the men, when a shell fell close by killing two men and wounding the C.O. and two others. The Colonel received two wounds, one on the crown of the head, and one in the right leg. He showed the greatest coolness and refused to be attended by the doctor until the wounded men were first looked after.

Our doctor now, by the way, was not our beloved Captain Cosgrove. He left us, broken down in health but universally regretted, two months before. His successor, Captain Beard, was an excellent chap also, most conscientious, very capable, devoted to the men, and a thoroughly good fellow.

To our extreme sorrow the Colonel was evacuated to hospital. Captain Roberts assumed command of the battalion.

We moved again to the front line on the night of the 18th and relieved the 54th battalion. On that day the following reinforcements marched in to our detail camp at Becourt :—Lieutenant W. S. Cooke, Second-Lieutenant Clift (cadet), Second-Lieutenant Baldry, and Second-Lieutenant Woolwrych.

On the 22nd May, two 16th battalion (A.I.F.) men, who had been prisoners in German hands for six weeks, escaped into our lines. The poor fellows were dead-beat. They had been treated with the greatest cruelty by the enemy, and were worn out in body but not in spirit. They entered our lines at 3.40 a.m., having eluded their captors. We sent them back to D.H.Q. A few weeks later they were returned to Australia.

We were relieved by the 54th battalion on the night of the 22nd. The relief was completed by 1.45 p.m. on the 23rd. We moved to the support line. There were only a few casualties.

The 12th K. R. R. relieved us on the 25th. We moved to Faireul for the night. We moved again next day to Bealencourt to the camp previously occupied by the 12th K. R. R.

From May 26th to June 15th we remained

at Bealencourt. We spent the time in reorganization and athletic sports. The men recuperated very quickly, and soon recovered their old dash and vigour. There were twenty-eight evacuations to hospital during this period, the chief cause being trench-fever. However, this disease had diminished very much by comparison with the previous month. In the opinion of the R. M. O. this was attributable to better conditions generally, and to frequent baths.

On June 15th we moved to Bouzincourt, having entrained at Bapaume. We were brought by rail to Varennes and marched from there to our destination.

Under the command of Major "Jock" Thompson, M.C., we were billeted at Bouzincourt until the 6th July. The other battalions of our brigade lived close by. In fact the whole division was quartered within easy reach, hence we had a gala time. Major-General Hobbs, the Divisional Commander, was most anxious that the men should obtain every facility for sports and healthy recreation. His efforts were seconded by every officer in the division, so that athletic competitions, concerts, and grand divisional sports were the order of the day. The weather was excellent. The locality was charming. To all intents and purposes so little were we disturbed by the cyclopean struggle being waged some thirty miles distant that the war might have been in another continent.

On the 6th of July, 1917, we moved forward, but not into the trenches. There was special training to be carried out by each brigade. The ground most suitable for the manœuvres was situated some miles from the town of Mailly. Our camp was close to this village or town. We lived in huts, and were tolerably comfortable.

While at Mailly Camp we had many convivial meetings and reunions. Captain Geoff. Street, Captain Norman Lovatt, Captain Tom Dick, Captain Pearson, and the writer seemed to drift together every evening, consequently those evenings were memorable.

Two important events occurred while we lived at the above-mentioned camp. Lieutenant (Bill) Lang gave Colonel Marshall of the 15th Brigade the knock-out blow, and so secured to the Green and Blacks the divisional heavy-weight championship. The other event of interest was the return of our beloved C.O., Colonel Croshaw. Didn't we give him a right hearty welcome? There wasn't a man in the battalion, from the Second in Command to the humblest private, who wasn't rejoiced at his recovery and reassured at his return. The general opinion with regard to his leadership was this: "With Croshaw with us, everything is bound to be right. With him away—well, we can't be so confident or cocksure." He had scarce been back a day when he resumed work with his old extraordinary thoroughness and indomitable energy. Those who had become slack in his absence got an electric shock, or, as the men expressed it, "they got it in the neck."

During the next few months the Colonel and I became more intimate than ever. I realized what a grand soul his was, and how big a part religion played in his life. Uninfluenced by me, except perhaps by association with me and other Catholics, he decided that it was his bounden duty to follow the light and be received into our Church. His reception occurred a few weeks before he fought his last fight and joined the glorious Deathless Army over Beyond. But I must reluctantly refrain from writing too much about him, and relate the further history of his grand battalion.

SECTION XI.

I have always been guilty of a certain regard for ne'er-do-wells. I am invariably standing up for them in the belief I possess that there are good qualities and noble traits in the worst of us. Kindness and consideration in my experience are far better reformative forces than severity and harshness. Indeed, in our Australian Army, the jack-boot system, when introduced, plays the very devil with the men.

In the Whale Oil Guards there were many heroes. Many of them, officers and men, were those whose private lives were without blemish, who were always amenable to discipline, and whose decalogue was summarised in the ideal they held up to themselves—" Play the game." And so we had our gallant Colonel " sans peur et sans reproche," we had Captain Charley Arblaster and Captain Jackson, Captain Johnson, as brave as he was blunt, and Captain Lang, as fearless as he was frank. We had too Sergeant-Major Monro, Sergeant Saunders, and many men in the rank and file whose souls were as free from cowardice as their records were free of crime-sheets; but there were others, some of the "bad-hats," who, in action, were the bravest of the brave, and who won distinctions, despite their chequered records, by the outstanding brilliancy of their deeds of gallantry and self-sacrifice. In time my estimate of men underwent a remarkable change. I grew to regard wildness and licentiousness not commendable but to a certain extent pardonable, while the unforgivable sins are cowardice and selfishness.

Among the officers there was Captain Bob Ramsay. Bob, while yet a Lieutenant, had been awarded the Military Cross for bravery in Gallipoli. In the line, there was no more capable company commander. He was a father to every man in his company. He understood Australians thoroughly, and though he maintained strict discipline, was perhaps the most popular officer in the battalion. In the trenches he never touched alcohol. His care for the men's safety and comfort won him the regard and admiration of the Colonel. In No Man's Land he was as happy as if he were stalking kangaroo in the bush of Queensland, and was as unconcerned under a machine-gun barrage as if it were only a summer shower-burst. In the line no officer was truer to his trust. Out of the line no officer was more irresponsible.

His escapades were nightly occurrences. Many of them were laughable in the extreme.

On one occasion he persuaded the driver of a motor waggon to give him a ride to Amiens. Bob's first care on arrival was to fill the unsuspecting Tommy with strong liquor and so put him out of action for at least twenty-four hours. The gallant Captain enjoyed himself thoroughly in that gay town for half a day, and then with his boon companions went for a tour on the captured motor-transport round that corner of France. He arrived home a a few days later and strange to relate escaped trouble.

Another night he had enjoyed himself at a neighbouring mess not wisely, but too well. When leaving, his host presented him with two bottles of Johnny Walker. The night was dark, so the redoubtable Bob found some difficulty in making his way. Near the guard-house he fell into a quick-thorn hedge. Try as he might, he was unable to extricate himself. He called out loudly and turned out the guard. The sergeant rescued him, and the Captain in gratitude presented him with one of the bottles.

Poor Bob was never so happy as when entertaining his fellow-officers at his company headquarters billet. As a host, he was inimitable, and many a jovial evening did he give us. There was much to be reprehended in his wild adventures, but his bravery and generosity endeared him to me, and so I shall ever remember him as a white man.

Among the men, how many of the incorrigibles were surprise parties in action?

For a long time a hopeless drunkard, Bluey Ward was the bane of Captain Murray's existence. Murray was the O.C. of B company to which Ward belonged. The unfortunate ex-batman was constantly up before orderly-room, and yet so well known to the officers were his good-nature and fearlessness that he invariably received light sentences.

I suggested to the Colonel that Bluey should be appointed a company stretcher-bearer. At the same time I succeeded in getting the fellow to promise that he would cut out strong drink. The C.O. was only too pleased to give him a chance to make good, with the result that Bluey became one of the most exemplary men in the battalion. Stretcher-bearing was his true vocation. The interest he took in his job, his bravery, endurance, and self-sacrifice were so outstanding that he very soon endeared himself to the men of his company. When he received the well-earned decoration of the Military Medal, Bluey was indeed a happy man. He now realized that he had a reputation to live up to, and so serious and enthusiastic did he become about his work that the boys began to accost him as Doctor Ward.

Many a time had I reason to feel grateful to Bluey during the winter of 1916. Often, when cold, tired and dispirited, did Ward come to my rescue with a steaming pannikin of cocoa or coffee. On such occasions his honest, ugly face seemed to me seraphic and his carroty head wore the glory of an aureola.

Another celebrity who liked the wine of the country too well when out of the line trenches was Sergeant Paddy Lonergan. He likewise was A1 in the trenches. He was one of the lucky ones who came back safe from Fromelles, but he had an undue conceit of his prowess in that affair and not only expected distinction, but promotion to the officers' mess. He was the last man any C.O. would recommend for a star, for he could never be even an honorary gentleman.

Before Fromelles, a friend of Paddy's, Sergeant John Ridley, afterwards a most popular officer, persuaded him to see the chaplain, and put his soul in order. Lonergan had primed himself for the coming battle with a more than liberal allowance of rum, consequently, when he did consent to visit his spiritual director he was scarce in a mood for pious exercises. Father Kennedy was standing in front of Colonel Norris's dug-out talking to the C.O., and several officers, when the redoubtable Lonergan made his appearance.

"Well, Sir!" the excited Irishman exclaimed. "Young Ridley would give me no rest until I promised to see you and go to confession. Well, here I am, Sir, and I've been every bloody thing a sinner could be, except a murderer."

The chaplain, though embarassed, laughed and replied "Very good, Lonergan, but the days of public confessions are past. Come to my dug-out and I'll attend to you."

After Fromelles, Pat did not receive the recognition he thought he was entitled to. As a result his libations were fierce and his permanent condition alcoholic. Captain Cosgrove and I well remember one evening at Fleurbaix when he harangued us on ould Ireland's wrongs, his own wrongs—another injustice to Ireland, by the way—and bade us good-bye as he was off to the enemy's lines to give away our "possys." Needless to say Pat went no further than the nearest estaminet.

Despite his predominant failings, he was a brave man. He finally succumbed to trench-feet, and the battalion knew him no more.

When making special mention of individuals, I must not overlook Captains Johnson, Jackson, and Lang.

No gathering of the officers was complete without Aubrey Johnson, or Uncle John, as we familiarly styled him. His blunt candour endeared him to all of us. His dry humour had a spice all its own. Many a sample could be given if these memoirs weren't concerned with more serious matters.

Aubrey was returning on one occasion from English leave. He could not find any Australian officers on the boat from Folkestone to Boulogne, so he joined a group of English subalterns. Johnson is rather a good-looking man. His face is tanned by exposure to the warm Australian sun, and is decidedly virile. When dining with his new friends at Boulogne, one of them, a lisping, pimple-faced youth, was rude enough to remark with an inane giggle. "Pardon me, old chap, for staring so at you, but you know you've got such a deuced hard face."

Johnson retorted good humouredly. "Oh you are welcome by all means. But now that I look at your dial, you certainly are no Gladys Cooper."

Captain Johnson was wounded several times and won the M.C. He was an officer who never lost his head, and so he always commanded the confidence of the men and of his brother officers.

Bert Jackson! No one will ever recall the Whale Oil Guards without remembering this magnificent boy-captain. His presence meant laughter and fun. Jacko, as we all called him, had no enemies. Oftentimes, though he worried secretly about his young wife and baby-boy in England, did he cheer us up when the days were dark and the conditions terrible. He came away with the first Australian

Division, was on Gallipoli, and severely wounded there, returned to obtain his commission, was wounded again at Fromelles and again recently. He is one of those about whom we all anxiously enquired after every stunt: "What of Captain Jackson. Is Jacko all right?"

He wears the Military Cross. It ought to be the Victoria Cross.

Bill Lang, another of our boy heroes! His real name is Jo, but Bill Lang was an Australian prize-fighter of some repute, so we called Jo Lang, Bill. Only twenty-two when he left us, he stood six-foot-three in his stockings. Some officers dubbed him Bill Longtitude. Captain Lang had been a Sergeant on Gallipoli and was wounded there. He was wounded again at Fromelles and returned to the battalion in the line before he was fit, so lonely did he feel away from his beloved comrades. If I ever knew a man who was absolutely fearless, that man was Captain Lang. When I qualify this statement by saying that he was the soul of honour, clean in soul and upright in all his dealings, you will understand Bill's popularity. The only occasions when Lang was unwelcome at a company mess was when the rations were short. His swallowing propensities were stupendous.

He, too, wears a well-earned M.C. He left us in December, 1917, for the Indian Army. We missed him sorely, but were glad that his brave career was not ended in the bloody shambles of Flanders.

Another officer, whose influence for good was immense, was Lieutenant Ridley. I do not belong to the same persuasion as Jack's. He is a Methodist. I am a Roman Catholic, but I say of him most sincerely that he is one of the most perfect Christians I have ever met. A mere boy in years, though he had passed through the ranks, he remained as pure and unsullied as when a schoolboy, inspired by patriotic enthusiasm and confidence in God, he had volunteered for service with the A.I.F.

Brave as the bravest, cool and manly in action, Jack Ridley was beloved by officers and men. There are many chaplains with the A.I.F., but I doubt if any of them has been a more successful teacher among the men of those virtues that make mortals Christ-like and heroic.

Captain Stanley Evers is another Anzac boy-officer to whom I take off my hat. Before the war he knew nothing of men. He had never been to public school, but was carefully educated by a mother who idolized him. Yet this mother's boy relinquished a safe staff job in order to share the risks and hardships as well as the glory of his Anzac comrades. Wounded twice during my career in the battalion he returned last April only to be severely wounded again. He. too, was one of those grand fellows who, though a soldier, was always a true Christian. Would to God we had many more such as he and Jack Ridley.

SECTION XII.

We left Mailly on the 16th July, and marched to a village called Rubempré.

Captain Pearson and I rode on ahead of the battalion by some hours. The day was warm and sunny. The country through which we cantered was very beautiful with its rolling downs, white villages, and spire-topped churches. Calm and pastoral it looked, and one found it hard to realize that some thirty miles away the war was raging and taking its toll of thousands of lives.

During our short stay at Rubempré we celebrated the anniversary of Fromelles. General Hobbs addressed us and gave us a hint that we were destined for fierce fighting in the North very soon. He also congratulated us on our achievements and told us that we would soon have an opportunity to avenge our comrades who died on the 19th July, 1916. While in this pleasant village the sergeants gave a banquet to the officers, and we returned the compliment by an open-air moonlight concert and supper to the sergeants in an enclosed orchard at the back of the headquarters billet. Both functions were the most enjoyable we had ever held.

On Sunday, July 29th, we entrained for the North. We travelled all night and detrained at 9 a.m., at Arques. From there we marched to Lynde, a distance of seven miles. In this village we were billeted until the 17th September.

The happiest time of our service was spent at Lynde. The village folk among whom we lived were simple kindly people, who welcomed our coming and appreciated our stay among them. There was ample time for rest, for recreation, and sport, for reorganizations and training, and for Church parades. The curé allowed the Roman Catholics of our brigade the use of his church, so our priest and men availed themselves of the opportunities afforded them by holding frequent services.

During our stay at Lynde Colonel Croshaw, after long previous consideration, decided to receive instructions preparatory to entering the Roman Catholic Faith. His friend,

Father Kennedy, gladly helped him and received him into the Church on September the 16th, just before we moved into the forward area.

Ah me! What halcyon weeks those were at Lynde! What sad and happy memories are associated with them! Almost every evening after mess, the Colonel and I strolled out for a walk along the lanes or through the pleasant harvest fields. The man disclosed his soul to me, his great ideals, his hatred of cant and hypocrisy, his reverence for what might be styled nowadays the oldfashioned virtues in women, his hatred of the modern woman—unsexed and un-natural, regardless of home-ties and motherly duties, blatant and raucous, clamouring for rights never intended for her in the Creator's scheme of the world's government.

Like most idealists, he had met with disappointment, consequently in his character there was a certain sadness. I really believe that his heart was in his battalion, and his happiest days were those spent on active service with us, Australians.

I have often mentioned in these pages that all good things come to an end in this sphere. So, too, did our happy time at Lynde. We moved out on Monday, September 17th, and marched towards the forward area as far as

Steenvorde. We marched on again on the
18th through Poperinge to a camp near
Reninghelst. We were now in Belgium.
The Ypres salient was quite near. The thunder
of the guns all day and all night long was
terrific. Enemy planes came over just after
we had turned in under our bell-tents and
bombed the town and the camps near by.
The alarm blew lights out. There was no
use leaving our tents, we might as well be
blown out of existence in them as out in
the open, so we remained where we were,
listened to the ominous drone of those death-
birds in the air, to the occasional crash of
the bombs they dropped, and the barking
of our anti-aircraft guns ; and hoped none
of their deadly souvenirs would fall our way.
This was a nightly experience during our stay
at Reninghelst.

We marched into supports on the evening
of the 21st September. Never shall I forget
that march. Colonel Croshaw and I walked
side by side for a considerable time. He
spoke to me about the officers he had sent
back to the divisional detail camp in charge
of the portion of the battalion detailed to
remain out of the line.

"Poor chaps," he said. "It grieves me
to leave them out. Nearly all are darned
good officers, the same is true of the other

ranks; but orders are orders. I could not take them all and I have made the selection in the interests of the battalion."

Then he said to me, just as Colonel Norris had formerly confided in me.

"K———, old chap. I am not a bit nervous, but I have a presentiment that this is going to be my last fight. I've felt it before we left Lynde, and to-day it is stronger than ever. Well, welcome be God's Will! All I pray for is that we may do well and that if I am to go, death may be instantaneous."

Our route lay by the ruins of Dickiebusch and by the outskirts of martyred Ypres. As we plodded on we noticed the good repair of the corduroy roads laid down away from the old highways in this war-cursed and desolate district. Ypres! Words cannot adequately describe its destruction. Once a prosperous commercial city with its world-renowned architectural gems—its Cloth Hall and Cathedral. Now it was a foul heap of crumbling ruins, a city shrivelled up with the terror of war, a place where the devilish Hun had vented his hellish rage, and on which he had belched the hate of his artillery and left his beastly mark.

Poor outraged Belgium! May God grant that defeat and shame may overtake your ghoulish oppressor, that the Kaiser and his litter of brutish princes with his Kultured generals may be made pay the price of their bloody deeds of lust, murder, and incendiarism.

When we had left Ypres behind and skirted that lake of death—Zillebeke—a squadron of Fritz planes swooped from the clouds down towards us. The Colonel ordered us to spread out as much as possible. It seemed certain that they would attack us either with machine-guns or bombs, and the road being open and exposed, many casualties seemed unavoidable.

Just as suddenly as the enemy planes had appeared, British planes circled down to engage them. We halted by the road-side and watched the battle. The Germans beat a hasty retreat. One Fritz plane crashed to the ground on fire. Another Fritz in his flight succeeded in setting fire to an observation balloon. The observers used their parachutes and descended unhurt in a field near by.

Wonderful the escapes in this war!

When we arrived at our destination, Half-Way House, we found no house but a labyrinth of foul-smelling and vermin-infested tunnels. Though, prior to our marching out from Reninghelst, we had been informed that there was sufficient shelter for a brigade at Half-Way House, we discovered the place packed with Artillery, Engineers, and other nondescripts. For us there was scarce room for one company. Our battalion, with the exception of headquarters and one company, was forced to spend the night in a miserable trench where there wasn't a single dug-out. The enemy shelled us through the night. Towards morning D company had twelve casualties, six of whom were killed. One platoon was detailed to work the pumps in our odoriferous tomb to save not only ourselves, but all the other rag-tag crowd down there from drowning.

The Colonel was furious. He tried to discover who was responsible for the presence at Half-Way House of so many odds and ends. Indeed he believed that a considerable percentage of our fellow-citizens in this subterranean Belgian hell were men who simply used it as a resting-place without the knowledge or consent of their officers.

On the 23rd D company again suffered heavy casualties. A party of us went to remove and bury the remains of six men who were killed by a shell. Their platoon officer knew who they were. Just as well for us, for there was no other means of identifying them. We had to shovel their remains on to a sheet of corrugated iron in order to remove them. They were like sausage meat, and the sight, inured as we were to the horrors of the trenches, was un-nerving.

On the evening of the 24th we moved up to the supports. We left C and D companies at Half-Way House. They were to join us later in the front line before the hop-over. We arrived at the sunken road where the pill-box, our destination, was situated. Again we found damnable congestion. The 54th battalion headquarters were in occupation, so we had to share the place with them. B and A companies had arrived also without casualties. We were barely settled in our new positions when the most violent bombardment I have ever experienced was commenced. A heavy shell got a direct hit on our pill-box. The explosion killed a signal sergeant who was engaged with the buzzer near a window. Two others out in the trench at the time were killed. All of us inside were thrown violently to the ground, so we thought 'twas the end of things.

All night long, without cessation, the enemy danced shells on and around that pill-box. The doctors used the left-end compartment of it as their dressing-station. There was no room in there for the wounded, so many a poor fellow waiting outside his turn to be dressed was blown to pieces ere we could attend to him.

Next day the bombardment continued. B company suffered very heavily. Captain Johnson brought Lieutenant Jennings in his arms down to the Aid-Post, but when we arrived we found poor Con's life extinct. We laid his body down outside until we could inter him. Ten minutes later 'twas blown to pieces by a shell.

'Twas a day and night of horrors.

About midnight we moved forward to the front line. Colonel Croshaw received Holy Communion before we left the pill-box.

The attack came off at 5.50 a.m. on the morning of the 26th. The barrage of fire put up by our artillery was terribly magnificent. So thick was it that one of our wags said he could lean up against it and light his pipe.

The last we saw of the Colonel was when he addressed the officers just before the advance. "Gentlemen, your men before yourselves. Look to your flanks. God bless you lads till we meet again." He had the satisfaction of seeing his battalion charge to victory, but he did not arrive with them. A shell burst short and gave him his passport to Eternity. Stretcher-bearers bore him back to the Aid-post at Clapham Junction, but he died soon after his arrival there. Victory was ours. Our men gave the enemy hell

THE WHALE OIL GUARDS. 129

and reached the objectives without sustaining many casualties.

Such was the battle of Polygon Wood and such was the end of the bravest soldier, the most God-fearing Christian, and the most perfect gentleman I have ever known. The Whale Oil Guards will know him no more in the flesh, but his brave spirit will always be with us.

We buried him near the ruined schools on the Menin Road outside Ypres. The thunder of the guns and the scream of the shells are his dirge.

May God reward his soul with Eternal peace and rest.

SECTION XIII.

The battalion came out of the line on September 30th. The officers and men were thoroughly exhausted after their long and fierce ordeal. The Colonel's death cast a gloom over all of us. For the time it seemed that all the enthusiasm and the vitality of the Whale Oil Guards had died with him, but it was not so. A few days rest, and we resigned ourselves to the inevitable, prepared to be just as loyal to our new C. O., Colonel Cheeseman, as we had been to our late beloved Commander.

Our losses in Polygon Wood were very heavy. Colonel Croshaw, Lieutenant Jennings and Lieutenant Corry were killed. Captain Ramsay, Captain Johnson, Lieutenant Waite, and Lieutenant Pettifer were wounded. Many of our brave N. C. O.'s and men went west. Among them C. S. M. Brauer, C. S. M. Loney, and Sergeant Shanahan.

The other battalions of our gallant brigade suffered even more severely. The Green and White's lost their brave young C. O.—Lieut.-Colonel Humphrey Scott, D.S.O., their Adjutant—Captain Chappell, their M. O.—Captain George Elliott, with several other officers and many men.

The Green and Purple's lost several company commanders, with other officers and many men.

Colonel Wood's battalion likewise lost heavily. However, their brave and sturdy C. O. was still spared to them. Very few officers in the A. I. F. have done better than Lieutenant-Colonel Percy Woods, D.S.O., M.C., An N.C.O. on Gallipoli, he had arrived at his present eminent position by sheer merit and conspicuous ability.

Captain Norman Lovatt, who formerly belonged to the Whale Oil Guards, but who had been transferred to the Green and Purple's as their Adjutant, did stupendous work in that stunt. Though he was not awarded a distinction, he surely earned a D.S.O., or another bar to his M.C.

Our Captain Roberts had taken command of the battalion when Colonel Croshaw fell. We were all confident that his fine work would receive recognition, and so our joy was genuine when a few weeks later the honours were published and Roberts was awarded the. D.S.O. Other awards were Captain Johnson, Lieutenants Elliott and Geldard the M.C.

Poor Bluey Ward was badly wounded. When stretcher-bearing, a Fritz plane swooped down over the trench and fired on the bearers as they ministered to the wounded. Poor Bluey was one of the victims.

Another old friend and most gallant officer who paid the extreme penalty at Polygon Wood was the O. C. of the Brigade Machine-Gun Company—Captain Tom Dick. Peace be to his brave soul.

It was my melancholy duty to report to the Brigadier—General Hobkirk—on the 30th. Colonel Croshaw had entrusted me with a message of a private nature to be verbally delivered to the General in the event of the Colonel's death. I was then as always courteously received by the Brigadier. He was very grieved at our loss. He and our beloved C.O. had been warm personal freinds. Let me pay tribute in passing to General Hobkirk. He was a regular officer attached to the A. I F. He had been in the diplomatic service in Rome and other European Capitals and was an accomplished linguist. An Englishman of that type to which I have already alluded in these pages, broad-minded, cultured and honourable, he appreciated us, Australians, and we respected and honoured him.

Until the 21st October we were in the line and the front area, then we moved to a camp near Dickiebusch. We moved again on the 25th to Connaught Camp near Abeille. We stayed here until November 4th, when we moved again to very comfortable billets near Outterstene. Here we remained until the 10th, when we marched forward again to a camp near Locre. On the 11th, we marched to Kemel, and on the 12th we marched into the support line. We moved into the front line on the 13th. The sector was near Wytschaete. On the night of the 14th, Captain Evers was wounded and evacuated. He had a narrow excape. A machine-gun bullet entered his head near the right eye and came out near his right ear.

From the 14th November until the 28th I shared a dug-out with the M. O.—Captain

Hawthorne—at the entrance to Lancashire Sap. On the whole we had a quiet time, so much so that my friend, Hawthorne, had frequent fits of the "blues," during which time he moved about restlessly, to the detriment of our Chippendale, vowing that he was "fed up" and "bored stiff."

On the 21st November Lieutenant Lane was accidentally killed.

We came out of the line on the 28th to a very comfortable camp near Kemel. Here we had excellent opportunities for organization. Here also we realized that our new C. O. was a worthy successor to Colonel Croshaw.

Lieutenant-Colonel Cheeseman is an Australian. His military career has been so far brilliant for he has not yet attained his 25th year. He wears the decorations of the Legion of Honour and the Military Cross. In physique he is a giant. He is well educated and broad-minded. Off parade he is a genial laughter-loving boy who delights in the happiness and good-fellowship of his officers. For him, should he be spared, I venture to predict a great future. The dear old battalion is, thank God, in good hands.

Towards the end of December, 1917, ill-health compelled me to sever my connection with the Whale Oil Guards. In March, 1918, continued ill-health forced me to retire from Active Service. Since then I have lived quietly, hearing now and again from my old comrades.

That the Whale Oil Guards have been true to their traditions, the following letter will prove :—

> France,
> *October* 19*th*, 1918.

From W. Cheeseman.

Dear K ———

Many thanks for yours of the 8th inst., which has just arrived. I really thought you had forgotten me, as this is the first word I have had from you for ages. The letter you mention having sent to me to Wandsworth Hospital I did not receive.

I am delighted to know you are so well and expect to return to Australia shortly. " Bon voyage."

We heard you were still very ill, so you can imagine the joy in the battalion when I gave them good news of you. . . . .

. . . . . .

Hawthorne is in England somewhere in one of the T. B's. He was gassed at the same time as I was.

The battalion has had a tremendously hard time lately and has suffered severe casualties, losing some splendid officers and men, a number of them, unfortunately, being old hands. The officers killed were Captain Johnson, M.C., Captain Wilson, M.C., Lieutenants Shearwood, Lamerton, Davies, Anslow, Althouse, and Ralph. It was poor Althouse's first stunt.

I can't tell you how upset we all are over those splendid fellows going west, but it is the fortune of war and has to be borne. Indeed, they can never be replaced.

Against the terrible losses, one has to count the magnificent honours the battalion has gained and the tributes of praise from all the commanders—from Army down.

In two stunts we captured about 400 prisoners, 100 machine-guns, 8 field guns and several minenwerfers.

Among the many honours gained are Major Murray, D.S.O., Captain Smith bar to M.C., Lieutenant Waite bar to M.C., Captain Wilson, M.C., Stenson, M.C., Clift, M.C., and there are a number still to come. Roberts has been awarded the French "Croix de Guerre." We have two men recommended for the V.C., and expect word about them any day.

From the above, the severity of the fighting can easily be judged, and when I tell you that two of our stunts were the capture of Peronne and the smashing of the Hindenburg

Line south of Le Catalet (both of which were done at 3 hours' notice), you will be able to imagine what we've been doing.

I could go on writing for hours about the glorious achievements of the men, but time and space will not permit. I can say without fear of contradiction that the battalion has never been better both from the point of view of morals and military efficiency.

. . . . . .

I have read your letter to most of the officers and have conveyed to them your good wishes which they heartily reciprocate.

Best of luck and all good wishes,

   Yours sincerely,

    W. CHEESEMAN.

So Captain Aubrey Johnson has joined the Glorious Deathless Army! Ah me! life scarcely seems worth living when we, the survivors in the Great Adventure, recall our illustrious dead. However, we must carry on until the call comes. If we have suffered privations and wrestled with death during the war, association with Australia's bravest and best has been ample compensation.

As I write this last page the clock strikes the midnight hour. The Feast of All Saints will be welcomed in a few hours by the blazon of church bells and the peal of swelling organs. I think on the glory of the Eternal City where God's triumphant followers celebrate their festival. Surely many of the men I knew, whose remains now lie mouldering in Flanders, walk in the glad procession. So I believe, and so I say : Oswald Croshaw ! Charlie Arblaster ! Colonel Norris ! Aubrey Johnson ! Norman Lovatt, and all my dead comrades of the Whale Oil Guards :

"Peace be to your brave souls."

THE END.

SPECIAL ORDER
BY
LIEUT.-COLONEL W. J. R. CHEESEMAN, D.S.O., M.C.

Commanding 53rd Battalion A.I.F.

8th December, 1918.

Under authority granted by His Majesty the King, the Field-Marshal Commanding-in-Chief has awarded the following decorations—

DISTINGUISHED SERVICE ORDER.
    Lieut.Colonel W. J. R. Cheeseman, M.C.
    Lieutenant R. V. Hill.

MILITARY CROSS.
    Lieutenant J. G. Ridley.

DISTINGUISHED CONDUCT MEDAL.
    1737. Sergt. Smith, C.
    3502. Sergt. Callaghan, R. L.
    2217. Pte. Newland, A. G., M.M.
    5371. Pte. Grocott, F. T.

The Corps Commander has awarded the following decorations :—

BAR TO MILITARY MEDAL.
    3489. Sergt. Croker, J. E., M.M.
    3259. Pte. Barron, E., M.M.

MILITARY MEDAL.
- 3372. Sergt. Adams, C. H.
- 4851. Sergt. Smith, W. H.
- 2474. Sergt. Quantrill, R.
- 3345. Corpl. Lynds, R. A.
- 3598. Corpl. Say, W.
- 3378. T/Cpl. Gledhill, H. R.
- 5465. T/Cpl. Taylor, C.
- 3252. L/Cpl. Boserio, W. C.
- 1643. L/Cpl. Phillips, J. E.
- 855. L/Cpl. Miller, T.
- 376. L/Cpl. Barnidge, R.
- 9182. L/Cpl. Mitchell, A. E.
- 5405. Pte. Lavery, W.
- 5331. Pte. Bartley, P.
- 3115. Pte. Bridge, H.
- 3493a. Pte. Black, J. D.
- 5437. Pte. Ramsden, J.
- 3498. Pte. Blackham, A. G.
- 2988. Pte. Walker, E.P.

The Corps Commander wishes to express his appreciation of the gallant services rendered by the undermentioned officers and O/Ranks who were "Mentioned" in Australian Corps Routine Order No. 49 of 3/11/18.

- Lieut. A. C. Elliott, M.C.
- Second-Lieut. P. E. Ralph, M.M.
- 5464. Pte. Sullivan, R. V.
- 3228. Pte. Allen, P. S.
- 2521. L/Cpl. Sinclair, P. R.

The Army Corps, Divisional and Brigade Commanders wish their congratulations conveyed to all the above-mentioned.

The C. O. also desires to add his congratulations.

A. C. ELLIOT, Lieut.
Adjutant 53rd Battalion A.I.F.

SPECIAL ORDER
BY
LIEUT.-COLONEL W. J. R. CHEESEMAN, D.S.O., M.C.

Commanding the 53rd Battalion A.I.F.

December 13th, 1918.

His Majesty the King has approved of the award of the following Decorations :—

VICTORIA CROSS.
    1584a. Pte. Curry, W. M.

Under authority from His Majesty the King the Field-Marshal Commanding-in-Chief has awarded the following Decorations :—

DISTINGUISHED SERVICE ORDER.
    Major J. J. Murray, M.C.

BAR TO THE MILITARY CROSS.
    Captain W. E. Smith, M.C.
    Lieutenant W. Waite, M.C.

MILITARY CROSS.
    Captain W. F. Lindsay.
    Lieutenant W. Bevan.
    Lieutenant J. Dexter.
    Lieutenant A. W. Cooper.
    Lieutenant A. J. Tofler.
    Lieutenant G. A. Young.

DISTINGUISHED CONDUCT MEDAL.

- 3487. T/C.S.M. Burns.
- 2962. T/C.S.M. Wood, J.
- 2153. Cpl. Crank, R.
- 2283. L/Cpl. Weatherby, C. J.
- 2247. Pte. Smith, O. W.
- 2642. Pte. Cameron, R. C
- 2768. Pte. Gilmore, H. J.

The Corps Commander has awarded the following Decorations :—

BAR TO THE MILITARY MEDAL.

- 1753. L/Cpl. Willard, H. E., M.M.
- 4875. Pte. Sullivan, J. S., M.M.

MILITARY MEDAL.

- 3498. Sergt. Croker, J. E. B.
- 3408. Sergt. Scully, V. J.
- 5406. Sergt. Lineham, C. C.
- 3256. Corpl. Baker, R. J.
- 1720. Corpl. Rayner, C. R.
- 5474. L/Cpl. Turner, A. J.
- 1142. L/Cpl. Brown, W. C.
- 5479. L/Cpl. Webb, A. G.
- 4852. L/Cpl. Smith, A. E. L.
- 3353. Sig. Alexander, A. J.
- 3427. Pte. Smith, E. J.
- 2444. Pte. Marsh, C. S.
- 2171. Pte. Greenhalgh, W. J.
- 5405. Pte. Lette, B. I.

THE WHALE OIL GUARDS.

1887. Pte. Clarke, G. F.
3259. Pte. Barron, E.
5390. Pte. Hopkins, A. J.
869a. Pte. Payne, A. C.
4662. Pte. Wilson, W. S.

The Corps Commander wishes to express his appreciation of the gallant services rendered by the undermentioned Officer who was " Mentioned " in the Australian Corps Routine Order No. 48 of 17/10/18.

Lieut.-Col. W. J. R. Cheeseman, D.S.O., M.C.

And of the undermentioned O/Ranks who were " Mentioned " in the Australian Corps Routine Order No. 47 of 22/9/18.

3582. Sergt. Sullivan, J. P.
1670. L/Cpl. Groves, W. J.
5437. Sig. Ramsden, J.
2988. Sig. Walker, E. P.
1421. Pte. McGrogan, J. C.
3228. Pte. Allen, P. S.

The Army, Corps, Divisional and Brigade Commanders wish their congratulations conveyed to all of the above-mentioned.

The C. O. also wishes to add his congratulations.

A. C. ELLIOT, Lieut.
Adjutant, 53rd Battalion, A.I.F,

13/12/18.

www.ingramcontent.com/pod-product-compliance
Lightning Source LLC
Chambersburg PA
CBHW032124090426
42743CB00007B/463